Swim,
Bike,
Run,
Laugh!

A Lighthearted Look at the Serious Sport of Triathlon and the Ironman Experience

by

Dan Madson

authorHOUSE™

1663 LIBERTY DRIVE, SUITE 200
BLOOMINGTON, INDIANA 47403
(800) 839-8640
WWW.AUTHORHOUSE.COM

First published by AuthorHouse 06/20/05

ISBN: 1-4208-4522-5 (sc)

Library of Congress Control Number: 2005903129

Printed in the United States of America
Bloomington, Indiana

This book is printed on acid-free paper.

Contents

Dedication

This book is dedicated to my wife Lisa. Without her support and encouragement I would not have written this book or done an Ironman triathlon in the first place.

When Ironman first came to Madison in 2002, I got up early on the day of the race and went to watch the start of the swim. Later that day I tried describing to Lisa how incredible it was, but she didn't seem very interested. She supported my initial training and attended my first five races during the summer of 2003 but probably didn't understand the dedication necessary to complete an Ironman-distance race.

The following September, when I started thinking seriously about doing Ironman, I convinced her to come and watch part of the race so she could see what I was so excited about. Lisa and I got up early and drove to the swim start. I explained everything that was about to happen as we stood on top of the Monona Terrace and Community Convention Center before the beginning of the race. It was thrilling to see 2,000 athletes begin swimming as the cannon sounded across the water, and that's all it took to get her hooked.

Later that afternoon we drove to one of the tougher hills on the back side of the bike loop. One after another, riders struggled up the climb on their second lap, many of them walking their bikes. One man walked stiff-legged and in obvious pain and discomfort. Later we found out that he was a type 1 diabetic competing in his first Ironman. Since our youngest son suffers from the same disease, this made an impact on both of us. It was inspiring to see this man struggle through the terrible cramps he was experiencing.

Finally we drove to the Capitol Square and stood for an hour at the halfway point of the run. We watched people reach the turnaround in varying moods. Some were glassy-eyed and somber as they shuffled around the marker and headed dejectedly back out onto the run course. Others jumped and kicked their heels and gave high-fives to people in the crowd as they made the turn. One guy stopped right in front of us, walked up to a race official who was standing inside the barricade, and started to cry. "I have to take myself out of the race," he said. The official put his arm around the man's shoulder and escorted him toward the medical tent. Lisa said, "I just wanted to reach over the fence and grab him and tell him 'You only have 13 miles to go!'"

As the evening wore on, Lisa and I sat in the bleachers at the finish line and listened to the announcer call the name and city of each finisher. "You did it!" he would say over and over again. "You are an IRONMAN!" It was an inspiring and moving day for both of us and the turning point for Lisa. From then on she supported my undertaking.

The next morning when registration for the following year's race opened, Lisa watched over my shoulder as I signed up, and I believe she was as excited as I was. She gave me the freedom to train as hard as I needed, and that included a lot of long weekend sessions. She pestered me about running, the weakest part of the sport for me. She got to know some of my training partners and traveled to all my races. And finally, she spent the entire day of Ironman Wisconsin cheering me on. When I crossed the finish line she was there to greet me and give me a great big hug. At 7:56 P.M. on September 12, 2004, a volunteer placed the finisher's medal around my neck—but it was really for both of us!

Introduction

Most of the books written about the sport of triathlon are pretty serious and straightforward . . . *Triathlon 101, Triathlon Training for Women, Triathlon Training on Four Hours a Week.* They all deal with obvious topics like swimming, biking, running, nutrition, and so on. They're filled with sample training plans, drills to fix technique problems, healthy menus, and physiological explanations of how oxygen is delivered to your blood cells, how glycogen depletion causes muscular fatigue, and why your lipolytic system works more efficiently when you are in good shape. None of them, however, seemed to address my personal needs. I looked and looked for books that related specifically to my life's situation but could find nothing like *Triathlon Training for the Married, Sleep-Deprived, Overworked Father of Three,* or *How to Do An Ironman Without Training at All.*

When I competed in my first triathlon in July of 1983 without any serious training, I didn't know that 20 years would pass before I would compete in another. Nor did I realize how that second race would initiate a personal Ironman quest that would end 16 months later as I lay on my family room couch with a finisher's medal around my neck, an immense feeling of accomplishment, and an IV tube stuck in my left arm.

The History of the Sport of Triathlon

You can credit whomever you like for inventing the sport of triathlon, but the fact of the matter is, I did! From the ages of 6 to 12 my neighborhood friends and I spent most of our days swimming, biking, and running, though not always in that order. In between those three activities we pestered our sisters, foraged for food in each other's refrigerators, and threw dirt clods at each other from across the street. Once school let out and summer vacation began, my friends and I were out the door early in the morning for cowboys and Indians, Batman and Robin, baseball, football, go-carting, or any other activity we could conjure up.

After lunch we tucked dimes into the pockets of our swimming suits, hopped on our bikes, and raced to the swimming pool, located in a downtown park adjacent to the river that skirted the edge of the city. From the highway to the pool parking lot there was a steep dirt path that had been packed hard by the wheels of a thousand bikes. We flew down that trail, kicking up clouds of dust, and just before reaching the battered bike stand we locked up our back brakes and fishtailed to a stop. We hopped off the bikes and racked them fast enough to make modern-day transition times pale in comparison and then sprinted to the entrance as each of us wanted to be the first to slap his dime on the desk in front of the lifeguard on duty. We spent many glorious afternoons splashing around the pool and lying on the warm concrete deck.

After supper we raced around the neighborhood on our bikes with baseball cards (including 1967 Carl Yastrzemski rookie cards) clicking and clacking against the spokes in our wheels. None of us carried USAT cards or wore race numbers. Bike helmets were unheard of, and spandex had yet to be invented. We were primitive triathletes in the heyday of youth.

To give credit where credit is due, I will mention a couple of other facts. The first *official* triathlon was held in San Diego, California, on September 25, 1974. The event featured a grand total of 46 men and women who had been persuaded by its founders to give this unusual race a try. The participants experienced 6 miles of running (longest continuous stretch, 2.8 miles), 5 miles of bicycle riding (all at once), and 500 yards of swimming (longest continuous stretch, 250 yards). Two miles of the running was to be done on sand or grass with no shoes, and participants had to bring their own bikes. The winner raced home in a respectable time of 55:44, and the sport of triathlon was officially born. The 35th-place finisher in that first event, John Collins, became the creator of the first Ironman Triathlon four years later.

One day Collins, a Navy commander stationed in Hawaii, had gotten into a heated argument over which athletes were in better shape, runners or swimmers. Since he had an interest in international cycling, he personally thought that cyclists were the best-conditioned athletes of all. Collins issued a challenge that he felt would settle the argument. His contest was an event that would combine three previously established races—the 2.4-mile Waikiki Rough Water Swim, the 112-mile Around Oahu Bike Race, and the 26.2-mile Honolulu Marathon.

Fifteen people agreed to attempt what seemed ridiculous at first. Twelve of the 15 finished the race, and the winner was Tom Warren, a 35-year-old from San Diego who completed the event in 11:15:56. *Sports Illustrated,* the lone magazine that covered the event, called it "lunatic."

In 1980 ABC's *Wide World of Sports* covered the Ironman and brought it to the attention of the world. That event was won by Dave Scott, a 26-year-old masters swim coach from Davis, California. He finished in 9:24:33, shaving nearly two hours off the previous winning time. Robin Beck won the women's division in 11:21:24, placing 12th overall. The second Ironman ignited enthusiasm for swim-bike-run events, and triathlons began to develop around the world.

Over the years a handful of names rose to prominence in the world of triathlon, namely as Ironman champions—Dave Scott, Mark Allen, Paula Newby-Frasier, Scott Tinley, Greg Welch. However, it was the stunning finish of Julie Moss in the 1982 Ironman championship that attracted the attention of people all over the world. A young college student, Moss, who had been leading the race, collapsed from dehydration and exhaustion 20 yards from the finish line. She was passed by another competitor but bravely crawled the final distance and somehow managed to finish the race. This emotional and inspiring conclusion lifted triathlon's popularity and triggered a boom in participation everywhere.

I spent 21 years teaching and coaching middle school students in Madison, Wisconsin. In my first year I was thrown into the deep end when I was assigned a class of 33 seventh graders, 29 of whom were boys. We met in a room that was designed to comfortably hold about 20 kids. With 33 growing junior high kids crammed in there, it became a day-by-day game of survival. Just the smell generated by 29 pre-adolescent boys whose personal hygiene habits were questionable should have been enough to prompt me to reconsider my career choice, but I hung in there and we learned from each other.

One of my first students was a boy named Jon Becker. His mother taught at our school, and he had a successful but unremarkable career as a student-athlete. In high school he did not play any sports, and after he graduated his mother informed me that his goal was to attend Harvard law school and become a lawyer. I was dubious about his aspirations but said nothing.

A few years later, after Jon had graduated from Harvard law, his mother told me at school one day that he was training for a marathon. As a longtime recreational runner I had to admit that I was impressed. I hadn't had any idea that Jon possessed the ability or the gumption to attempt a formidable distance like that. I didn't even know that he liked to run. A couple of years later, Jon's mother let me know that he had started doing triathlons and was planning to compete in the inaugural Ironman Wisconsin to be held in Madison.

It didn't come as a surprise to me that Madison had been selected as a site for an Ironman event. The downtown sits on an isthmus between two beautiful lakes. There is tremendous support for athletic events of all types. In addition to great weather and a beautiful countryside, Madison has a very active multisport community. What surprised me was that Jon was going to be one of the participants.

I had always wanted to see an Ironman race, so I went. I watched the start of the swim and spent the rest of the day on the Internet tracking Jon's progress. He ended up finishing 307th overall with a time of 11:20 in only his second triathlon. That did it. I called him and we had a long talk about his training. I asked him as many questions as I could think of and decided that if he could become a triathlete and complete an Ironman, so could I! With that thought in mind I quickly realized that the first thing I needed to do was . . .

Chapter 1
Set Some Goals

Everybody Else Will Think You're Crazy

The first thing you have to do in order to become a triathlete and complete an Ironman is set some goals. In my wife's business, her motto has always been, "Your goals should be so big that when you tell your friends and family, they laugh at you." Employing that philosophy, I said, "Honey, I would like to be a triathlete, train 40 hours a week, complete an Ironman, and qualify for the world championship in Hawaii." She started laughing. I took that as a good sign, but left my goals open for revision.

How did I know that goal setting was important? My parents used to tell me all the time. "Have you set any goals for the summer?" they asked each year when school let out for the last time.

"Yeah," I answered, "I'd like to sleep until noon every day and when I wake up I'd like a duffel bag full of hundred dollar bills waiting for me on the end of my bed." Most of my teachers, coaches, and even a few of my friends also talked about goal setting. None of my friends ever actually seemed to have any goals, but they all thought that I should.

Numerous books with imaginative titles like *How to Set Goals* and *Goal Setting Is Important* and *How to Set Important Goals* have been written on the topic. Companies spend millions sending their employees to goal-setting workshops to help the employees comprehend that if they learn how to set goals they will become more productive. In most cases, all this does is help them achieve one of their most common goals: Avoid Going to Work for a Couple of Days.

As a result of all the early encouragement I received, I thought it would be appropriate to state the goals I have in writing this book. They include the following:

1. Provide myself with a new excuse to skip some long training runs.
2. Address *significant* questions that a triathlete contemplates when sitting in a porta-potty before an Ironman race: Is it really necessary to put Vaseline on my nipples before the run? How can I tell if my kidneys have failed? What should I say to the people just coming out of T2 as I'm finishing the race?
3. Give something back to the sport of triathlon, which has given me more than I could have ever imagined, including an appreciation for the delicate art of leg shaving, the joy of getting up at 5:15 in the morning on a regular basis, and that persistent feeling that no matter how much training I have done, I haven't done enough.

I've always set big goals even though I haven't written them down or even verbalized them. I just knew there were certain things I wanted to accomplish and acted accordingly.

For example, when I was in fourth grade I knew that I wanted to get Gloria Hemme's attention and somehow get her to like me. She was the most beautiful girl in the class and I had a massive crush on her. I was too scared, of course, to actually talk to her, but I did let it slip to one of my friends that I kind of liked her, and he told my other friend, and that guy told one of Gloria's friends, who told another one of her friends, who I think might have told her. I'm not certain she ever got the message. I realize now it's possible that as the message was passed from friend to friend to friend it could have morphed from "I like Gloria Hemme" to "I biked far on Wednesday" to "I had pie for breakfast." Since I didn't know for sure if Gloria had gotten the message I continued to work toward accomplishing my goal.

One morning at recess, my friend Gary and I snapped some long thorns from a thorn tree that happened to be growing on our school playground. Why anybody would plant thorn trees on a grade school playground still mystifies me. In any case, we twisted two of the longest, sharpest thorns from the tree, concealed them in our pockets, walked over to the bike rack, and proceeded to pop both of Gloria Hemme's bike tires. I was fairly certain that this would get her attention, and I was right.

After school that day I saw Gloria crying as she walked her bike toward her house 11 blocks away. My friend Gary was walking next to her, pleading for her to stop, and I assumed that he was trying to pin the blame on me. She never once turned and looked at him. She stuck her chin out and looked straight ahead while guiding her disabled bike.

The next morning we discovered that we had gotten someone else's attention, because both Gary and I were called to the principal's office during morning recess. Gary was a frequent visitor to the principal's office and didn't seem to be too concerned about this invitation. On the other hand, I had *never* been to the principal's office, and I was petrified. We were escorted by Mr. Griffin's secretary to his office. As we stood there I realized that not only had we popped Gloria Hemme's bike tires, but I had also forgotten to wear a belt to school that day, and belts were mandatory apparel for the boys. I had heard rumors of spankings and ear-pullings that had me shivering with nervous fear. As I stood before Mr. Griffin I noticed that my shirt was partially untucked, and then I saw him glance at my waist. At that point I did what most fourth grade boys would do in my situation—I started bawling.

I was crying so hard that when Mr. Griffin said, "Boys, do you have anything to say for yourselves?" I just started babbling, coughing, and hyperventilating, all at the same time. "Mr. Griffin, I couldn't . . . sob, sob . . . find my belt when I got up . . . sniffle, this morning . . . sob, sob . . . and I'm sorry for popping Gloria Hemme's bike tires . . . sniffle, sniffle . . . Up to this point Gary had been standing there stone-faced. When I admitted to the deed without even having been pressed, he turned and glared at me as if to say "That's not how things work in here."

"Boys, after school today the two of you will walk to the hardware store, buy two new tires for Gloria's bike, and put them on for her. Is that clear?"

"Yes, Mr. Griffin," I said.

After we fixed her tires, Gloria Hemme never spoke to me again. She had never spoken to me before either, but now I was fairly certain that my chances of getting her to like me were pretty slim.

When I started high school my parents continued to talk about setting goals like getting A's in all my classes, working hard in sports, and being kind to everybody.

I suppose these were admirable goals to pursue, but during my freshman year my only goal was to draw and color Mr. Eaton's neckties. I had noticed during the first week of geometry class that Mr. Eaton never wore the same tie, and he had some pretty cool ties. I decided that since I didn't understand half of what he was talking about anyway, I would spend my time in his class sketching and coloring the tie he wore to class that day.

3

I kept two notebooks for geometry class, and by the end of the first semester the one that should have been filled with completed assignments was mostly empty, while the other one was filled with 87 carefully drawn and beautifully colored neckties, none of which were identical. I always wondered what Mr. Eaton's closet looked like. Did he start with tie number one at the beginning of each semester and work his way through his collection again? I got a D in geometry, but when I showed my drawings to my art teacher she was impressed.

In college my goal-setting ways continued. I was used to my mom washing all my clothes when I lived at home. It seemed to me that she spent an awful lot of her time in the basement washing, drying, and folding clothes. When it dawned on me that I was now responsible for this task I knew I wanted to spend as little time as possible in the dormitory laundry room. My first goal in college, therefore, was to wash my sheets and bedding once a semester. I put brand-new blue and white pinstriped sheets on my bed during the first week of football practice in August and didn't wash or change them until Christmas. As the weeks of school progressed, the sheets gradually changed from crisp blue/white to dingy blue/brown. The pillowcases had unidentifiable spots and discolorations on both sides and matched the new hues of the sheets. About halfway through the semester I revised my goal and turned the pillowcases and sheets inside out.

As you can see, goal setting has always come naturally to me. When I saw my first Ironman triathlon on ABC's *Wide World of Sports* in 1980 I was impressed by the fit bodies of the competitors, amazed by their determination, and intrigued by the peculiar mix of joy and suffering I witnessed—but I couldn't envision myself ever doing something like that. My goal at that time was getting a certain college cheerleader to notice me without having to pop her tires.

Two years ago when I began entertaining the thought of doing an Ironman I realized that I might have to update some of my goals. Consequently, my first goal was to . . .

Chapter 2
Learn How to Swim

Chlorine Will Eventually Eat Large Holes in Your Swimming Suit

My mother used to say, "If people were meant to swim, they would have been born with fins." Her aversion to the water was legendary. When our family went on summer vacations we always begged her to come into the water with us. On one occasion after hearing these persistent pleas from her children, she reluctantly agreed to give it a try.

Her swim apparel included a conservative one-piece suit and a stretchy yellow swim cap with a chin strap that pulled the flaps down tight over her ears and helped keep her hair dry. Not that her hair stood much of a chance of getting wet, as it rarely got closer to the water than three feet. We cheered and splashed her. She kept saying "Don't you dare get my hair wet!"

We pleaded with her to put her face in the water and try to swim. She finally gave in. She closed her eyes, cupped her hands, put her arms into stroking position, and slowly leaned forward to place her chest and face into the water. She put one hand forward to attempt her first stroke and promptly sank to the bottom. We rushed over and pulled her up from under three feet of water. She spluttered and shook her head while she tried to clear the water from her eyes. "If people were meant to swim, they would have been born with fins!" she cried. The swim cap proved effective, however—her hair never got wet.

Even though Mom didn't care much for the water, she insisted that her kids take swimming lessons. Going to the pool by ourselves and swimming all afternoon was a lot different than taking swimming lessons. Swimming lessons started at 8 o'clock in the morning when the air was still cool and the water was downright cold. Mom drove us to the pool and hustled us in all wrapped in towels, goose-bumped and shivering.

Our swim instructor Molly the Lifeguard didn't like it any better than we did, but she had an advantage . . . she never had to get in the water. She wore a baggy, hooded sweatshirt, wrapped a huge towel around her waist that hung almost to her feet, and taught the entire class from the concrete deck of the pool while we froze. Swim class always started the same way. "OK, kids, sit on the side of the pool and kick your feet to get warmed up." We kicked half-heartedly and got angry with whoever splashed water on us. "Now, everybody jump in!" Molly shouted cheerily. *Extra* cheerily, since she knew she wouldn't be joining us in the Arctic water. "Everybody dunk their heads under now!" she shouted. We looked at each other sullenly, gathered our courage, plugged our noses, and took the plunge. Oh, that water was cold! We shot from the depths like missiles, the air literally knocked out of our lungs.

Gradually, we warmed up and dutifully completed all the silly little drills that we were instructed to do by our teacher. As much as I hated them, the lessons did equip me with some rudimentary swimming skills that paid off in the afternoons. In order to be able to swim in the deep end or jump off the diving boards, you had to be able to swim the width of the pool twice without stopping. I managed to complete that simple test the first day of each summer, much to the chagrin of my friends whose mothers did not force them to take lessons.

I developed a love for the water during those early days in the public swimming pool, but I never actually swam laps. Our swimming consisted mainly of jumping off the diving boards, playing tag, and getting yelled at by the lifeguards for running on the deck. They constantly shouted "Slow down! NO RUNNING! You're going to fall and hurt yourself!" Funny thing, during all the years I was there I never saw one kid slip and fall.

One day I made a breakthrough in my swimming technique. I was by myself at the shallow end of the pool when I decided to experiment with my stroke. I leaned forward, pressed downward, and actually started swimming. It was not the head-up, combination front crawl/dog paddle stroke that I usually used to navigate short distances in the pool, but an actual swim stroke. I practiced for about five minutes and then, satisfied that I had mastered the sport, hopped out of the water, sprinted across the deck, climbed the ladder to the top of the high board, and did a beautiful cannon ball with Miss Lifeguard's warning trailing faintly behind me. "Hey, Danny, NO RUNNING! You're going to fall and hurt yourself!"

Decades later, when I decided that I wanted to become a triathlete and needed to start swimming distances, I did what any 43-year-old man would do—I bought myself a Speedo and joined the YMCA. I had worn a Speedo only once before, on a Jamaican vacation. Lisa had seen me walk out of the bathroom dressed in a rainbow-colored Speedo, and the coffee she had just sipped sprayed out of her mouth. "Are you planning to wear that to the beach?"

"Well, yeah," I said. "What's the matter with it?"

"Oh, nothing," she said as she turned away laughing.

She wasn't the only one who found my attire impressive. I turned quite a few heads that day as we walked to the beach. I realize now that this may have had something to do with the fact that the portion of my thighs between the bottom of the Speedo and where my golf shorts normally hung had never been exposed to the sun. It was a soft, smooth, pale expanse of virgin skin. And after five hours under a tropical sun, that skin was seared tomato red. I put the Speedo away.

Now, while talking to Jon, my former student who had done Ironman, I asked if he knew of any books that would help me plan some swim workouts. He suggested that I read a book by Terry Laughlin called *Total Immersion*. Appropriate title, I thought, considering what I was about to get into. I really didn't expect to learn how to swim by simply reading a book, but I did find *Total Immersion* very interesting. In fact, I read it cover to cover twice and tried to digest all the new terminology and memorize the two-letter abbreviations for drills and sensory perceptions explained in the book like RA (Right Arm), LA (Left Arm), CU (Catch Up), DH (Down Hill), RW (Reach for Far Wall), and WA (Weightless Arm).

I was eager to get in the water to practice, so I typed out the first skill-builder, sealed it inside a little baggie, and headed off to the YMCA pool for my first practice session. I'll never forget how great it felt to be back in the water. I stretched my swim cap over my head, adjusted my goggles until they were snug, and pushed off from the wall. I felt really strong the first 25 yards. I reached the far end of the pool, turned, and pushed off again. By the time I was halfway back my already shaky swim stroke had started to degenerate. As I plunged into oxygen debt, I quickly turned into a thrashing, inefficient mass of flailing limbs and began gasping for breath. I realized that this was going to be harder than I had thought. I got out of the pool and sat down with the book, ready to reevaluate my first practice. At this point, I thought Mr. Laughlin could have added a few more abbreviations to his practice list, like CB (Can't Breathe), MS (Must Sneeze), and IQ (I Quit).

As I sat there I watched a woman swimming laps. Superior athletes always seem to make their sports look so easy, and good swimmers are no different. She glided effortlessly down one length of the pool in eight strokes, flipped, turned, and cruised back to the other end. Back and forth she went, methodically stroking lap after lap.

A good swimming stroke is like a good golf swing—both require many different muscular movements, and in order to train your muscles to remember those movements automatically you have to repeat the movements over and over again. The fact that my golf swing memory has Alzheimer's and my scores can range anywhere from 75 to 115 didn't bode well for my future as a world-class swimmer, but I decided to get back in the water and talk myself through some stroke cues. I ducked under, pushed off, and began to swim again while trying to mentally focus on every technique I could remember. *Elbow up, relax head, press buoy, weightless arm, snap hips, breathe deep, swim downhill.*

I reached the end of the pool and realized that I still had three or four cues to recite. I cleared my head of all information and started back with only three words replaying over and over in my head—relax and swim . . . relax and swim . . . relax and swim. Gradually I found a rhythm. My heart rate calmed, my breathing relaxed, and I actually began to feel pretty good. When I looked at the girl in the lane next to me, however, I realized that she was swimming three lengths for every two of mine, and I knew I still had a lot of work to do. I struggled through 36 laps that first workout and exited the water exhausted, with a sore right shoulder to show for my efforts.

As I practiced over the next couple of weeks, I tweaked some things in my stroke and made some progress but still didn't feel as though I was swimming very fast. One day while I was in the water I noticed a man at the side of the pool helping another swimmer with his stroke. After the swimmer left, I got out and went over. "Are you by any chance a swimming instructor?" I asked the man.

"I sure am," he said, "I teach a master's swim class here."

"How would you feel about giving me some free advice?" I asked.

"I'd be happy to," he said. "Jump back in and swim 200 yards for me."

He walked alongside the lane while I struggled through four laps. When I climbed out of the pool he began listing some of the things he had noticed about my stroke. "Your head is too low in the water. Your right arm crosses over the center line of your body on every stroke. During your pull you push down on the water, which lifts your body upward instead of propelling it forward. You aren't rotating your hips and upper body enough. Your breathing is too shallow. Your elbows are entering the water before your hand. You aren't gliding far enough on each stroke. Your turnover is a little too slow. Your legs are too low. Your body fishtails in the water, and your kick is very weak."

"Is that all?" I asked.

"All for now," he said.

Boy, I was encouraged!

"Tell you what. I'm usually here at this time every day. If you want me to teach you a few things, I'd be happy to work with you after my class is done."

"I'll be back tomorrow," I said.

He followed through and turned out to be quite helpful. He seemed to keep an eye on me during many of my practice sessions. One day as I was climbing out of the pool, I got the feeling he was frustrated with me even though I was trying as hard as I could to incorporate his instructions into my swim stroke. In my mind I understood all the things he explained to me, but I wasn't always able to put them into practice. As I hoisted myself onto the deck he looked at me. "Do you have attention deficit disorder?" he said.

I laughed. "No! Why would you think that?"

"Oh, I don't know," he said. He grabbed some skin on my belly. "Have you been eating enough?" he asked.

"I eat all the time," I said.

"I worry about you overtraining."

I laughed again. "I'm always looking for excuses to get out of my workouts. That's the last thing you have to worry about with me," I told him.

I wasn't quite sure where his line of questioning was headed, but I took his last comment as a compliment, as if he thought I was trying hard even though I wasn't mastering everything he told me. I swam for an hour three times a week those first few months and began to feel more and more comfortable in the water.

Before Christmas of 2002 I started shopping for a wet suit. I knew from watching triathlons on TV that most triathletes wore them. I thought this was mainly for warmth and knew that would be important in Wisconsin, since the first race I had scheduled would be in early June when lake temperatures still hovered around 60 degrees. I didn't realize that a wet suit also increased buoyancy, which in turn increased speed and decreased leg fatigue.

I stopped at a couple of bike stores before I found one that had a decent selection. I took a short-sleeved Ironman Stealth wet suit into the changing room, stripped down to my running shorts, and started pulling the thing on. I squirmed and struggled. By the time I had both arms and legs inserted, I was dripping with sweat in the stuffy little booth. When I finally emerged, I said to the salesman, "This suit doesn't feel comfortable at all. I think it must be the wrong size or something."

He started laughing. "Actually, the reason it doesn't feel comfortable is because you have it on backwards. The zipper is supposed to be in back."

I marched back into the changing room, peeled the wet suit off, put it on the other way, and sure enough, it fit like a glove. After six weeks my swimming stroke was developing slowly but surely, and I was the proud new owner of a wet suit. I knew it was time to . . .

Chapter 3
Buy a Nice Bike

Don't Be Surprised If You Have No Money Left to Buy New Running Shoes

If you walk through the transition area of a triathlon you quickly realize that the machines parked there are not your father's bicycles. Most of the futuristic frames have names that bring to mind images of violent speed—names like Javelin, Litespeed Blade, Kestral Talon, Felt B2. They rest on top of feather-light, black carbon wheels, with blunt names like Hed and Zipp, that are aerodynamically designed to slice through the wind. Simply stated, they are weapons built for one purpose—to deplete all existing money from your bank account. If you bought just a frame, you might get away for something around $1,000. But the frame needs parts— expensive parts made of high grade aluminum, carbon, and titanium. The parts connect to wheels that are often as costly as the frame. Massed in one staging area, these bikes have a combined value that exceeds the gross national product of some small countries.

My first bike cost $15, and I remember it vividly. In fact, I remember every bike I ever owned. When my parents took pictures of us kids they often had us stand next to our bikes. "When you look back on your childhood," they explained, "you will be able to place each time in your life in relation to the bikes you owned."

I had just turned 6 years old when we moved to the small town of Luverne in southwestern Minnesota in 1965. The only bike in our family was a prehistoric fat-tired behemoth that must have weighed 75 pounds.

Not only was it impossible for me to ride, it was impossible for me to hold up once the kickstand was retracted. Fortunately for me, there was a 12-year-old girl named Anna Olsen who lived next door, and she owned a 26-inch girl's bike with no cross bar. Even though the bike was taller than I was, I could still stand on the pedals inside the frame and propel the bike forward.

I learned to ride by coasting down the sidewalk in front of the houses on our block. I cautiously rolled from one end of the block to the other, walked the bike back to the beginning, and did it again. On my fourth or fifth trip past the house where Anna lived, I began to feel more confident. She stood at the bottom of her front stoop with her arms folded and watched me. As I picked up speed I turned to look at her and took my right hand off the handlebar to wave. Just then the front wheel hit a crack in the sidewalk, the bike swerved, and I veered headlong into a huge elm tree that grew on the boulevard. The bike stopped immediately, but I kept going. It was a picture-perfect illustration of Newton's Third Law of Motion—an object in motion tends to stay in motion. I was the object that stayed in motion, and my crotch took the brunt of the blow.

Upon impact, the bike shuddered momentarily and then slowly tipped over with me draped over the handlebars. All the air was expelled from my lungs with an audible "Ooofffff," and for the first time in my young life I experienced the type of pain that only a boy or man can comprehend. It was a crushing, dull ache that started in my groin and slowly radiated downward into my thighs and upward into my belly. I lay back on the grass, squeezed my eyes shut, clenched my fists, and tensed every muscle in my body. I thought I was going to die. When I finally opened my eyes, Anna was standing right above me. I couldn't tell if she was more concerned about me or the fact that the front wheel of her bike no longer held a shape that was remotely circular. All I know is that she didn't let me ride her bike anymore after that incident.

The next summer my older sister Becky and I both asked if we could get our own bikes. My dad didn't have enough money to buy both of us new bikes, but he found an elderly man in town who rebuilt, repainted, and sold bikes. Today we would call them "pre-owned," but back then they were referred to as "used." We drove to this gentleman's house and were escorted into his basement workshop, where we were allowed to pick from the handful of bikes in various states of repair. I ended up choosing a 24-inch clunker with wide tires, no fenders or kickstand, and a dull orange paint job. It was heavy as a tank but mobile, and it only cost my dad $15. My sister chose a boy's bike with a thick cross bar, shiny silver fenders, and a roomy wire basket bolted to the front of the handlebars. Hers cost

$20 and I was a little jealous that my dad spent more money on her bike than on mine.

Dad drove off in the car as we hopped on our new rides and started home. I arrived first and waited for my sister, who didn't come and didn't come and didn't come. Eventually I saw her limping down the street crying. Her hands and knees were skinned raw and bleeding. "What happened?" I asked.

"My bike broke in half," she cried.

Dad came out of the house and asked the same question. "What happened?"

"I was riding down the street and my bike just broke in half!"

After Dad and I attended to my sister's road rash, the three of us hopped into the car and drove back to the spot where my sister's bike lay. Sure enough, there it was in the middle of the street in two chunks. Her frame had literally cracked in half right down the middle. I picked up the front of the bike while Dad put the back in the trunk, and we returned to the man's fix-it shop to demand a refund. He took the bike back and promised to weld the two pieces of the frame together. From that day on I rode in endless apprehension that my bike might suffer the same fate. I became determined to somehow earn enough money to buy a brand-new bike the next summer.

That fall I convinced my parents that I was old enough to have a paper route. I told them of my plan to earn money to buy a new bike and surprisingly, they agreed. I signed up with a paper route manager named Mr. Drury and spent the next nine months delivering 30 copies of the *Minneapolis Star-Tribune* to houses in our neighborhood every day after school. Not only did I have to deliver the papers, but I had to collect money from all the customers on my route. It was my responsibility to pay for my paper order every two weeks, and then I got to keep any extra money that I collected. It was not uncommon to have to make multiple stops at some customers' homes in order to get paid, but the memory of my sister's bike lying in two pieces in the middle of the street fueled my persistence to collect from everybody.

There were two customers that I never collected from. An elderly lady died and it was a month before anybody told me to stop delivering her paper, and one guy owned a big, ornery German shepherd that scared me to death. Despite my less-than-perfect collection percentage, I consistently earned $15 to $20 a month. After paying Mr. Drury every other Saturday, I would straighten out all the remaining bills, organize them by denomination, and hoard them in a blue zippered money bag that I secreted in my underwear drawer next to my bed.

Since there were no bike shops in our town, the next spring we drove to Sioux Falls, South Dakota, a 30-mile trip from home. I walked into a Schwinn bike store with a wad of cash stuffed in my front pocket and surveyed the huge selection of brand-new bikes. After some serious contemplation, I walked out of the store wheeling a Schwinn Stingray with a beautiful metallic-green paint job, high handlebars, a banana seat, and a flat racing slick for a back tire. The purchase set me back $69, but it turned out to be the best $69 I ever spent. From the time I was 8 years old until I got my driver's license, I logged thousands of miles on three different Schwinn bikes. Eventually a beat up Ford Pinto replaced my last bike, and the joys of riding faded from my memory.

When Lisa and I moved to Madison in 1982 so I could start my new teaching job, neither one of us had a bike anymore. I thought biking would be a great activity for the two of us to do together, so, without consulting her, I took what was left of our wedding money and paid a visit to a bike shop in downtown Madison. I had no idea what to look for, but I picked out a Nishiki road bike for Lisa based on the single criterion that it looked about her size. The guy that helped me with mine performed what I thought at the time was a pretty sophisticated fitting. He had me stand over the bar of a Bianchi road bike, then lifted it up, and estimated that since there was about an inch of play before it hit my crotch, it should be a pretty good fit. With the money I had left over I bought two helmets and a couple of strong bike locks. I didn't have the wherewithal to buy any of the fancy biking clothes that I had seen others wearing—padded shorts, cleated shoes, and tight-fitting, colorful jerseys.

Lisa and I rode together a couple of times, but I found that the pace we rode was not rigorous enough. When our daughter Rachel was a toddler, I attached a baby seat to the back of Lisa's bike and we tried riding as a family. The first time Lisa dismounted with our daughter on the back, the uneven weight of the bike caused it to fall over, and our one-and-a-half-year-old was ejected onto the lawn in front of our apartment building.

The next time we went for a ride we switched bikes so I could be responsible for our daughter's safety. Lisa could barely get on my bike, and as she wobbled into the street she nearly hit a parked car. I followed her on the route that took us around a nearby golf course. We stopped near one of the ponds on the course to feed the resident ducks, and as soon as I had dismounted from Lisa's bike, the weight of the baby seat unbalanced the back end again and Rachel tumbled onto the grass. From that day forward, every time Rachel saw us getting our bikes ready to ride she started crying, and frankly, at that point, we wondered how safe it was to carry our child on the back of a bike. We decided we would wait to resume family rides until she could ride along with us in a couple of years.

Whenever I could find time, I would head out and ride by myself for an hour or two, never feeling very comfortable on the bike but enjoying it nonetheless. At the time we had only one car, and since Lisa worked in a different city, I was forced to take the city bus to school or ride my bike. The first couple of years, whenever it was warm enough, I chose the latter mode of transportation. I presented quite a picture as I rode the busy streets of Madison in a suit and tie, wing tips strapped into the cages on my pedals, heavy book bag balanced on my back.

I have always subscribed to the philosophy that a clean bike is a happy bike, and I kept that bike spotless, cleaning and oiling it after every ride. It served me well for nearly 12 years until I had my first serious mishap. Coming home from a ride one afternoon, I hit a funny concrete hump on a side street and took a head-over-handlebars tumble. I suffered some scrapes and bruises while my bike suffered a fatal crack in its front fork. At that time I didn't have the money to repair or replace the bike, so I hung it in the garage and it's been there ever since, collecting dust.

Still, every time I saw bikers out on the road I thought back to the rides I had done and knew that a day was coming when I would be back out there with them. It happened in a rather unusual way. About a month after I had started swimming, I woke up in the middle of the night with a horribly sharp pain in my left elbow. After an hour of listening to me moaning and groaning in bed, Lisa had had enough. She forced me go to the emergency room to have it checked. When the ER doctor got to me, I could tell by looking at him that he was either a runner or a biker. His name was Shawn O'Brien, and he had the chiseled, lean, angular features often displayed by endurance athletes. I took a shot in the dark. "You must be a biker or a runner," I said.

"Both," he said matter-of-factly. "I do triathlons."

"You're kidding," I said, "I was thinking about trying the sport myself but have no idea where to start looking for a good bike."

"I'll give you the name of the guy that fit me and sold me my bike," he said.

After recuperating from the infection that had settled in my left elbow, I gave that guy a call. We scheduled a fitting appointment, and I saw Craig Watson for the first time the following week. As it turned out, he was part owner of a shop called Cronometro that specialized in building triathlon bikes, and he had a great reputation as a bike fitter. I introduced myself and asked what I thought was a simple question. "Do you think you could help set me up with a decent tri-bike?" Three and a half hours later, I had my answer.

"Looking at your size I think we have a couple of bikes that might work, but I think the Cervelo P2K is going to work best for you. It's a great bike for the money. It comes with a TrueAero aluminum frame with rear wheel cutout, 700c wheels, adjustable seat tube geometry, an aero carbon seat post, a full set of Ultegra parts, Velomax Vista wheel set, and Syntace Streamliner aerobars. It comes with an 11-23 rear cassette, but if you're planning to ever do Ironman Wisconsin, you might want to also get a 12-27."

I had no idea what he was talking about, so I asked the only question that came to mind. "Ah, like, how many gears does it have?"

"Eighteen."

"Cool."

Craig fit me with shoes first, adjusted the cleats, put me on the bike, and started taking measurements. He measured; I pedaled. I stopped; he adjusted. I pedaled; he watched. I stopped; he measured again. "How do the shoes feel?" he asked.

"Pretty good, I think," I said.

He put me back on the bike and started measuring again. Measure, pedal, watch. Off the bike, adjust. Back on the bike. Down into the aero position, pedal, stop, measure, adjust. "How does that feel?" he asked again.

"It's hard to get a deep breath when I'm down in the aerobars," I said.

He added a spacer to raise the aerobars. Back on the bike. Pedal, stop, measure. Adjust, pedal, watch. After three hours of measuring, adjusting, observing, taking notes, and asking how it felt, Craig finally said, "I think we've got it. I'll send you home with this setup and then have you come back after a month of riding to see how it's going. We can dial in the fit once you get a feel for the bike."

"OK," I said. He rang up the final sale for everything. I handed him most of my life's savings and headed out the door as happy as I had been 35 years earlier when I walked out of a bike shop wheeling a $69 Schwinn Stingray.

I had a million things to do when I got home, so, like the responsible adult that I am, I disregarded them all and went for a ride. I wriggled into my new bib shorts and jersey, strapped on my helmet, buckled my shoes, and took off. Soon after I left our neighborhood I climbed a gentle hill to a four-way stop. I unhooked my left foot from the pedal as I came to the intersection, but I leaned a little too far to the right. I felt myself slowly tipping and tried to put my right foot down to stop the fall. I couldn't, of course, because it was still clipped to the pedal. My life flashed before me as I slowly fell over with a crash. There were cars backed up at all four stop signs, and as I scrambled to untangle myself and stand up, I knew that everybody who saw me must have been thinking the same thing—"What a knucklehead."

I vowed I would never make that mistake again as I inspected the bike and my body for damage and headed off. I rode for an hour that first day and returned by the same route as the sun set in the west. As I approached the same four-way stop near my home, I was a much smarter rider. This time I unclipped my right foot as I came to a stop, but for some reason, instead of leaning to the right, I lost my balance again and felt myself tipping to the left. Same result . . . other side. There was a new audience in a different batch of cars, but the same thought was undoubtedly flashing through their minds.

By now I had a good start on swimming, I was perched on a brand-new bike (with a few small scratches), and I knew that it was time to add the third piece of the puzzle. I had to learn to . . .

Chapter 4
Become a Faster Runner

It Is Possible to Run Faster If You Just RUN FASTER

If ignorance were a salable commodity, I'd be rich. When I first entertained the thought of becoming a triathlete, I assumed that the run portion of the sport would be my strong suit. After all, I had been a recreational runner for nearly 25 years. Not a great runner, mind you, but nevertheless a runner. I was partly influenced by my dad, who would often ask, "Do you want to come up to the track and watch me jog?" I accompanied him every so often and can still picture him jogging around the high school track in his old black sweatshirt with the sleeves cut off, a baggy pair of brown corduroy pants, and a beat-up pair of tennis shoes that he wore when he mowed the lawn. While he jogged I kicked a football back and forth or threw a baseball against the brick wall of the high school and fielded grounders from myself. It seemed to take him an awfully long time to run around that track eight times.

Even though I didn't come from racing stock, I can honestly report that as a kid I was always the *second* fastest runner in my class. My friend Gary (see chapter 1) was always faster than I was and somehow got stuck in my class every year throughout grade school.

I grew up playing the traditional all-American sports—football in the fall, basketball in the winter, and baseball in the spring and summer. Consequently, I wasn't used to running fast for much more than 90 feet at a time. I'm ashamed to admit it now, but I always thought the long-haired skinny kids who ran cross-country and track were a bunch of sissies at the bottom of the sports food chain.

Yet when I graduated from high school, I became a recreational runner. It wasn't because I enjoyed running that much or because I was particularly good at it. I just thought it would be the best way to avoid getting fat.

The decision was one I had made after a Friday night football game during my senior year. As we left the field that night, a couple of former players were standing at the sideline. They had to have been no more than a year or two out of school. But I noticed that they had big, fat stomachs that hung over their belts. I wondered how and why they had let themselves go so quickly after high school.

That summer I bought a cheap pair of Nike running shoes and started running a mile-and-a-half route that I had measured out on the roads where I lived. Throughout college, when I wasn't in the middle of a sports season, I kept at it. When I started teaching in my early 20s I was still in reasonably good shape and wasn't afraid to tangle with my students on the playground. We had some epic kickball, touch football, basketball, and dodge ball games on the blacktopped playground. I caused my fair share of tears and bruises and sent more than a few kids to the secretary for medical attention. It was easy to forget that I was the adult and that I was playing with people half my age and less than half my size.

During the spring of my first year of teaching, in 1982, a college buddy named Scott called and asked if I wanted to run in the first annual Crazylegs Run that was to be held in Madison. It was a 5-mile road race named in honor of Elroy "Crazylegs" Hirsch, former NFL star and athletic director at the University of Wisconsin. Its purpose was to raise money for the athletic department at UW-Madison. I said, "Sure, why not?" Scott came down in late April, the Friday before the race, and we sat around and talked about old times and had a few beers. He had been a miler in high school and was significantly faster than I was.

Madison is a sports-loving city, and the turnout at the first Crazylegs Run was huge. After we registered on the morning of the race, we milled around the Capitol Square, amazed at the thousands of runners who had signed up for the inaugural event. A few minutes before it started, an old red fire truck pulled up to the starting line. Bucky Badger and a dozen cheerleaders were piled onto the back of the vehicle, and Elroy sat in the middle of everybody, square-jawed and smiling as always and sporting his distinctive flat-top haircut. We jostled our way to the front of the crowd where the elite runners were supposed to start. Scott and I stood next to a lean young runner with #1 pinned to his shirt. "Hey, good luck, number one," I said.

He looked at me, glanced at my race number, and said, "Good luck to you too . . . number three thousand, six hundred forty-five."

Races weren't chip timed in those days, so if you started way back in the pack, whatever time it took you to get to the starting line was added to your final total. Neither Scott nor I wanted to be carrying extra time baggage when we crossed the finish line. Just before the race started we shook hands and Scott said, "Hey, we should run together."

"Sounds great!" I said. Crazylegs fired the starter's gun and we were off. Scott disappeared from view before we rounded the first block, and almost immediately I was passed by a surging flood of runners. This tide of humanity, which included little kids, big dudes in high-top basketball shoes, senior citizens of both genders, and college kids who had probably just got in from partying, kept swerving around me until I was appropriately placed in among those people who ran at my pace. Needless to say, I wasn't second fastest in this race. Scott ran a sub-30-minute time, which placed him in the top 100 overall. I prefer not to reveal my finishing time.

That single race each April became the focal point of my running calendar. Scott and I ran in it every year with nearly the same results, and our standing joke at the starting line became "Hey, we should run together this year!" One year I decided to put in some extra time training, and I did manage to lower my fastest previous time from 37:56 to 37:50. I was pretty excited about that. When I got home I did some quick math and calculated that for every 20 miles of extra running I had done in the previous weeks, I had shaved one second off my time.

When I decided to pursue my midlife dream of becoming a triathlete I knew it would require discipline. I knew that the training would be long and solitary. I knew it would take time to build a solid base of fitness and get into racing shape. I knew that there was a good chance I could embarrass myself. I sat down and decided to . . .

Chapter 5
Organize a Race Schedule

Packing for a Race May Take Longer Than the Race Itself

My wife and kids say I'm anal retentive. I prefer to think of myself as "focused." They don't understand that there is a right way and a wrong way to load the dishwasher. They don't appreciate that each drawer in their closets should hold only *one* category of clothing. One day I took them all out into the garage and showed them exactly how to center their cars from front to back when they returned home and parked. They weren't amused. Now they purposely pull into the garage and park their cars as close to the front wall as possible just to see me get riled.

At the beginning of January 2003, in an effort to provide focus for my training, I registered for five races for the upcoming summer, the first scheduled for June 8. I didn't have a training plan. I didn't have a coach. I developed my own workout schedule based on how I felt on any given day. If I felt like running, I ran. If I felt like swimming, I swam. If I felt like biking, I biked. If I felt like skipping my workouts, eating an entire pizza, and washing it down with a hot fudge sundae, I did. Every so often I planned a brick session to get used to the feeling of going from swimming to biking or biking to running. Throughout the winter I trained mostly by myself and thought of nothing but that first race.

At the beginning of May I downloaded a map of the course and drove to Rock Lake in Lake Mills to preview it. I always found when training that the more times you swam, biked, or ran a route, the shorter it seemed to get. My goal was to do the entire course at least three times before the race.

In mid-May, the water temperature in Rock Lake was in the high 50s, and in my first attempt at swimming the quarter-mile distance, I lasted about 30 seconds. The shock of the cold was stunning and I had to gasp for breath. The blood in my extremities fled to my core, and my hands and feet went numb. I turned back, stumbled out of the water, and decided to focus on the bike and run courses instead.

I rode 15 miles, ran 3.1, and returned home satisfied that I was ahead of the game. I returned to the race site two more times. I found that the water had gradually warmed up and got to know the course like the back of my hand. The week before the race I sat down at my computer and generated a categorized checklist that contained 61 different items to pack on race day. Looking back, I realize that I was seriously overprepared for a race that would take me about an hour and 15 minutes, yet at the same time I didn't want to repeat the mistakes I had made 20 years earlier.

I had competed in my first triathlon in 1983. I had seen something in the sports section of the local paper advertising the event and thought, "How hard could it be to swim half a mile, bike 30, and run 6.2?" Based on the limited time I spent practicing in our apartment pool, I estimated that I could finish the swim in about 15 minutes. I had no odometer on my bike, but figured I could average around 30 miles an hour if I really pushed hard. I had never run 6.2 miles for time, but based on my Crazylegs race time I thought I would be able to finish the run in 45 minutes.

The race was scheduled for the middle of July, and I started training in June after I finished my teaching duties. I practiced swimming three or four times in the small outdoor pool at our apartment complex and had a terrible time keeping my cheap swim goggles sealed around my eyes. Water kept leaking in, and I had to stop every other lap to clear, readjust, and tighten them. I still couldn't afford biking shoes or shorts, and my running shoes were broken down and full of holes.

A couple days before the race I said to Lisa, "Hey, I was thinking about trying a triathlon this weekend." She knew me well enough to realize that if I said I was thinking about it I had already been thinking about it for a long time and had probably already registered for the race.

"Is that where you bike and run and swim? Why didn't you tell me about it before this?" she asked. "I told my parents we would come for lunch."

"I don't know," I said. "I wasn't sure you'd be too excited about it because it starts pretty early. And actually you swim first, then bike, and then run."

"Well, I don't care if you do it, but I'm going to take the car to my parents' house," Lisa said. "Where is it and how will you get there?"

That presented a bit of a problem. "It starts at Warner Park on the north side of Madison," I said, "and I guess I'll just have to bike down there and ride home after it's over."

After a pause, she said, "Have you even practiced for it?"

"Sure," I said, "I swam in our pool a couple of times and I've been running a bit. I really don't think it will be that hard. I figure it will take me about two hours."

"Whatever," she said.

I took her nonchalant answer as tacit approval, and it didn't bother me at all that she was not interested in coming to watch the race. She had paid her dues. She had sat through more football, basketball, and baseball games (doubleheaders included) than any girlfriend or wife should be expected to tolerate. The fact that she was planning to take the car didn't quell my enthusiasm one bit.

On the morning of the race I biked 7 miles from the east side of Madison to the north shore of Lake Mendota. I crammed all my stuff in a backpack and carried it on my back to the race site. The fact that I felt pretty tired when I got there was lost on me in the excitement of what I was about to undertake. The transition area was very informal. All the participants had their things laid out next to their bikes, which were spread out haphazardly on the grass next to the beach.

I checked in and then mimicked what everybody else was doing. I saw some people stretching, so I stretched. I saw other people running slowly to loosen up, so I ran for a few minutes. I saw most of the people arranging all their fancy biking gear next to their bikes. Since I didn't own any fancy biking gear, I just walked behind a big oak tree and took a leak instead. Almost all the racers had nicer bikes and better equipment than I did, but I was just excited to be there.

The excitement didn't last long, however. Right before the race was to begin, I walked down the beach toward the water in my baggy swimming suit and tried to tighten the elastic on my goggles. As I slipped the goggles over the top of my head to see how they fit, the rubber band snapped, rendering them useless. Nobody even looked at me as I tossed them aside, and I figured that I would just have to swim without goggles.

Even with a relatively small field, it was still crowded on the beach as the starter's horn sounded and people started walking out toward deeper water. I watched the people ahead of me and realized that I could walk for quite some distance before I had to start swimming. With no goggles, I decided to take advantage of the shallow water and walk as far as possible.

Finally, as the water crested my shoulders, I had no choice but to start swimming.

I put my head down and began stroking with my eyes closed. I quickly became disoriented and put my head up to see where I was going. I started again, this time with my eyes open in the water, and found that to be just as difficult. My eyes hurt, and I was struggling to breathe, so I started to use a panicky breaststroke in order to keep my head out of the water. What I thought would be a 15-minute swim turned into a 35-minute nightmare of breaststroking, side stroking, and floating on my back.

I was one of the last people out of the water. I realized at this point that I had no idea what I was doing. I watched as those ahead of me changed from swim suits to biking shorts with total disregard for the fact that they were momentarily naked in front of the spectators. I slipped a pair of gym shorts on over my swimming suit, struggled into a T-shirt, laced up my running shoes, and wheeled my bike toward the beginning of the second stretch of the race. My heart was hammering as I began pedaling.

Unfamiliar with the bike course, I tried desperately to overhaul the last few riders who were quickly pulling away into the distance. Within a few miles I had settled into a reasonable pace, though it certainly wasn't the 30 miles per hour that I had predicted. It was probably half that. As I started climbing the first big hill on the route, I had to stand up in a low gear just to keep moving while other riders flew past me seated and spinning as though they were on flat ground. It was a brutal ride. Somehow I managed to finish the bike course, but I was way at the back of the pack.

I stumbled off my bike and let it drop onto its side in the grass. My legs were burning from the effort, and I had very little desire to run 6.2 miles. I seriously considered quitting, but as I walked out of the transition area I heard some encouraging words from the small crowd of bystanders. "Hey, buddy, you can do it. You're looking great!" It would be the first of many times I would hear that notorious but well-intentioned lie.

I walked the first quarter mile before I recovered enough to start running. I settled into a pitiful jog haunted by a single thought . . . *I want to go home!* Not many people were behind me when I got off my bike for the final transition, and most of them passed me on the run. I managed to finish the run in slightly over an hour and dropped to the ground exhausted. I didn't care about my overall time. I didn't care about the T-shirt somebody handed me. I didn't care that many of the faster people had probably already packed up, gone home, showered, had a cup of coffee, read the paper, and taken a nap. The rest of the competitors were milling around drinking water and eating bagels and fruit. They were comparing finishing times and congratulating each other. I sat by myself, and my only thought was "How am I going to get home?"

I walked my bike to a gas station two blocks from the race site with the intention of calling home to see if Lisa was still there and ask her if she could come pick me up. I lifted a pay phone to my ear before I realized that I didn't even have a quarter to pay for the call. There was not a soul around from whom I could borrow money. I leaned my bike against the phone and sat down on the curb to assess the situation.

After resting for 10 minutes I hefted my backpack onto my shoulders, climbed back in the saddle, and began the long ride home. I had nothing left. As I slowly pedaled along, I realized that I had been foolishly optimistic in my predicted finishing times. It had taken me nearly three and a half hours to complete the event, and I knew that my lack of preparation had not only cost me a respectable finishing time but most of my dignity as well.

When I got home I suffered one final embarrassment. We lived on the second floor of the apartment complex, so I had to carry the bike up two flights of steps to our door. Standing outside the apartment, I realized that I had forgotten my key. I heard sounds coming from inside, so I knocked weakly, hoping Lisa would answer. She opened the door and surveyed me from top to bottom. "You don't look so good," she said.

"Yeah, thanks. I don't feel so good. I wanted to call you to come and get me but I couldn't find a quarter, so I rode home. To make matters worse I forgot to bring my key."

"You're lucky I was still here. I got a late start and was just about ready to leave. Now you can come with me."

"Sure," I said. "Do I have time for a shower, some breakfast, and a nap?"

"No!" she said. She was not amused. "Well, was it fun?" she asked. I detected a sardonic tone in her voice.

"I wouldn't exactly say it was fun," I said. "I think I should have trained harder."

"I could have told you that," she said. "Now hurry up. My parents are expecting us."

After my initial humiliating encounter with the sport of triathlon, I resumed my sporadic schedule of running and biking and busied myself with other pursuits.

Twenty years later, on the night before my first race of the summer of 2003, Lisa and I stayed at a friend's home in Lake Mills to shorten the morning drive to the race site. I set the alarm for 4:30 and went to bed early while everybody else stayed up.

Saying that my wife is not a morning person is like saying a root canal without Novocaine is not much fun. It's the epitome of understatement. Yet Lisa was determined to get to the event location in time for the start of the swim. My friend dropped me off at the transition area with the promise that he would return with Lisa and my youngest son Kyle in a couple of hours, and I saw that I was one of the first people to arrive. My bag was so heavy that I had a hard time carrying it and walking my bike at the same time.

I racked the bike on an inside lane of the transition area and started to unpack my equipment. I put down towels, laid out my biking shoes and socks, got my wet suit and goggles ready, filled a small bucket with water to wash the sand off my feet, topped off my water bottles, checked the laces on my running shoes, and had something to eat. I was first in line to pick up my race packet, pinned the race number to my tri-suit, went to the bathroom, stretched, went for a five-minute run, came back to my bike, and realized that I still had an hour and 15 minutes before the start of my wave. By now, the transition area was filling up with nervous racers, many of whom were first-timers like me. Jon, my former student, arrived and found me busily rearranging the stuff next to my bike.

"Hey, how do you feel?" he asked.

"I'm nervous," I admitted. "But I feel like I'm ready."

Jon had just arrived and was looking for an open spot where he could park his bike.

"How long have you been here?" he asked as he noticed that I looked pretty well organized.

"Oh, I got here shortly after 5:00. I wanted to make sure I had everything organized."

He laughed and then proceeded to give me what turned out to be the worst advice I had received up to that point.

"It's your first race. Don't worry about your time or where you finish. Just try to have fun."

Actually there were only two things I *was* worried about—my time and where I finished. I dismissed Jon's solicitous suggestion and went back to rearranging the things that I had just rearranged.

Finally it was time. I waded into the chilly water of Rock Lake with 51 other racers in the 40-44 age group. The starter counted down from 10 seconds, and all the racers pulled their hands out of the water and simultaneously started their stopwatches just as the horn sounded. I dove in, quickly found some open water toward the head of the pack, and started stroking as fast as I could. The pre-race jitters disappeared immediately and I went into a focused survival mode.

My plan was to go as hard as I could from the start until I crossed the finish line. I made two left turns, pulled toward the last buoy, and exited the water a minute faster than I had expected to. I pulled my wet suit partially off while running toward the transition area and kicked out of it as soon as I reached my bike. I mistakenly thought that it was necessary to wash the sand off my feet and put on socks before getting on the bike, and that wasted valuable time.

I pulled out of the transition area and started hammering as hard as I could, passing dozens of slower riders in the first few miles. I completed the out and back course in slightly over 40 minutes, changed shoes, and left the transition area for the second time.

This was the first time I had run after pushing as hard as I could on the bike, and I felt like Frankenstein for the first half mile. I struggled through the run as fast as I could. As I turned the last corner and headed toward the finishing chute, Lisa saw me. She started cheering. "Run faster!" she yelled. "Run faster! Don't let that guy pass you! Run faster!" I thought I had been running pretty fast, but apparently she thought differently.

I glanced back and saw a man about my age trying to track me down. I added a burst of speed as I approached the finish line, barely managing to hold him off. We were both gasping for breath after a strong finish, and we bent over next each other in an effort to regain our composure. I turned and looked at him. "Nice finish, buddy," I said. "Another 100 yards and I think you would have caught me."

"Yeah," he said. "I had you in my sights the last half mile but just couldn't run you down."

"You're the only one," I said. I had finished in 1:16:25, and as I anxiously searched the results, posted on the side of a truck, I was surprised to learn that I had finished fourth in my age group. I had narrowly missed a top-three finish. Jon found me. "Great job!" he said. "Hey, you got a fourth-place finish!"

I wasn't all that confident in my ability after only one race. "Do you think it was a fluke or was it a weak field?" I asked him.

"Actually, I think it was a pretty weak field," he said.

His honesty didn't dampen my excitement, however, and I celebrated with a bottle of cold water, a couple of bananas, and a big plate of French toast.

Over the course of the summer I learned something new in each race that I completed.

***

Lake Mills: 500-yard swim, 15-mile bike, 3.1-mile run
Finish: age group—4/52; overall—81/689
I learned that . . .

1. putting on socks after the swim wastes valuable transition time,
2. when the porta-potty lines are too long and the race is about to begin, it's possible to whiz in a wet suit without anybody noticing if you stand in the grass, and
3. the field *was* weak.

My best friend Kevin Castro started triathlon training about the same time I did. We have always had a healthy, competitive relationship and try to beat each other in everything we do whether it's golf, ping-pong, pool, or backgammon. We raced together for the first time in Lake Mills and I beat him by a couple of minutes. After the race, Lisa took a picture of us, and I was captured on film holding up four fingers in front of my body to remind Kevin where I had finished. Lisa warned me that this might serve as motivation for him to beat me the next time we raced. She proved to be right later that month when we raced together a second time in our first Olympic-distance event called the Amphibian Triathlon in Delavan, Wisconsin.

***

Lake Delavan Amphibian: 1,500-meter swim, 40K bike, 10K run
Finish: age group—12/43; overall—77/492
I learned that . . .

1. swimming in dirty water makes me sneeze,
2. I needed to improve my running, and
3. I would never do this race again.

Kevin and I had prepared together for our second race. We spent a morning previewing the course the week before the race and found that the water in the lake was like sewage. Kevin was a stronger swimmer than I was, so this distance suited his strengths. On race day I got out of the choppy water after a slow swim, and as I ran up the beach I saw Lisa and Nancy, Kevin's wife, on the beach cheering. As I ran past them, all I said was "Is Kevin out of the water yet?"

My wife yelled, "He was out five minutes before you! Hurry! You can catch him on the bike!"

I thought I could make up five minutes on the bike, but as I returned to the transition area after 25 miles I still trailed Kevin by 30 seconds. I hopped off the bike, changed shoes, and left T2. I was scowling as I passed Lisa and Nancy at the start of the run. "Where is that duffer?" I said.

"He's 30 seconds ahead of you," my wife yelled.

Later I learned that Nancy had looked at Lisa and said, "They're sure competitive, aren't they?"

I faded badly on the run, ended up losing ground, and ultimately finished five minutes behind Kevin. Once again—just as in our first race—the run had proved to be my weakness, and I vowed that I would improve my run time.

***

Madison Classic: 500-yard swim, 16-mile bike, 4-mile run
Finish: age group—6/20; overall—81/296
I learned that . . .

1. my swim times were getting better,
2. I always passed a lot of lower wave numbers on the bike, and
3. a lot of those same people always passed me back on the run.

We had a family gathering at our place that weekend, and some of the relatives came to watch the race. None of them had ever seen a triathlon before. They were pretty excited for me as I exited the water in the front of my age group, held them all off on the bike, and finished the run in a respectable time. My swim and run times were improving, and I felt encouraged by my results. I experienced a feeling of nostalgia as I began this race, as it had been the site of my first attempt at the sport 20 years earlier.

***

Waupaca Area Triathlon: half-mile swim, 20-mile bike, 3.1-mile run
Finish: age group—11/54; overall—68/539
I learned that . . .

1. this distance suited my strengths,
2. the 40-44 age group continued to be a very tough division, and
3. my run splits were still too slow.

I discovered that the perfect triathlon for me would be one that had a medium-length swim, a long bike, and a short run. Since the bike portion of each race had been my strongest leg, this race fit me perfectly. I passed a large number of people on the bike, as I usually did, and with a shorter run, not as many strong runners had time to pass me back again. Even though I felt I had had a strong race, I finished 11th in my age group and was disappointed. Near the finish, a fellow competitor coasted past me. "Where are you from?" I asked him.

"Madison," he said.

"Me too," I said. "Go get 'em!" I would meet him again sooner than I expected. As it turned out, he was a member of the training group that I was destined to join that fall. He was John Hollenhorst, a 51-year-old age-grouper who routinely finished in the top three of his division in races around Madison.

***

Devil's Challenge: 500-yard swim, 15-mile bike, 3.1-mile run
Finish: age group—7/69; overall—35/703
I learned that . . .

1. triathlons will be held even during a pouring rain,
2. I should have previewed the course as I had done before, and
3. falling tree limbs can be hazardous on the bike route.

This was my last event of the summer. On the morning of the race we awoke to the sound of a steady rain. As Lisa and I drove in the dark to Devil's Lake, I wondered if the race would be canceled. When we got there, the parking lot was already full of vehicles, and people were unpacking their gear and getting their bikes ready.

"Apparently these events are held rain or shine," I said. I felt bad about dragging Lisa out of bed at 5:00 in the morning, and now she would have to watch the race in a driving rain.

"Apparently," she said.

The rain continued to fall as we started the swim, and it never relented. So far this was the only course I had done that I had not previewed beforehand, and as I mounted my bike I was sorry that I had failed to make the effort. The first hill coming out of T1 was long and steep, and this was the first time I had seen people walking their bikes that early in a race. I crested the first hill with my heart pounding and my legs burning. The lenses in my glasses were amber colored, and with the raindrops falling I could barely see. I finally had to remove the glasses and tuck them in my shorts since I was riding without a shirt.

Coming around a bend on a downhill portion of the bike course, I noticed a commotion ahead of me. "Slow down!" somebody yelled. "You're going to have to get off your bike to go around." A huge tree had been uprooted in the storm and had fallen directly across the road a quarter mile in front of me. A couple of bikers had been forced to take evasive action, and one of them was hurt. The rest of us carefully made our way around the branches and continued onward. On the downhill portions of the course I could hardly see with the rain stinging my eyes. I put my head down and squeezed my eyes tight, without closing them all the way, and barreled ahead as fast as I dared. Even with waterlogged shoes, I managed my fastest run time of the summer that day. I crossed the line dripping wet but feeling strong.

My first season of racing was over, and I was encouraged by my progress. I knew, however, that if I was going to continue to improve and prepare for an Ironman I had to . . .

Chapter 6
Find Some Training Buddies

*Locating a Training Group That
Makes You Feel Inferior*

When I feel strongly about accomplishing a goal, I'm usually pretty dedicated. Let's say, for example, that I feel strongly about taking a nap. (This is something that I tend to feel strongly about nearly every day.) I will lock all the doors, turn off the phones, and eliminate all distractions that might prevent me from falling asleep for 40 minutes in the middle of the afternoon. Triathlon, like napping, is usually a solitary endeavor.

I've done most of my training by myself, and that can be both good and bad. The good part about training alone is that I can go whenever I want. I don't have to wait for anybody and I don't have to worry about others waiting for me. I can train early in the morning, in the middle of the day, or at night if I feel like it. The bad part about training alone is that I can go whenever I want. I don't have to wait for anybody and I don't have to worry about others waiting for me, but there's also nobody to hold me accountable.

I'm usually pretty dedicated when it comes to honoring my training schedule, but I also have developed a fairly extensive list of excuses to get out of a workout. The list includes, but is certainly not restricted to, such things as . . .

1. I'm tired.
2. My feet hurt.

3. It's raining.
4. My legs are sore.
5. It's too early.
6. It's too late.
7. I don't feel like it.
8. I just ate.
9. I'm hungry.
10. I need a nap.

After my first year of training and racing I realized that I needed to find a group of triathletes to train with if I was going to prepare for an Ironman event. Even though I had been modestly successful training by myself, I knew that there was a lot to be said for the dynamics of training with a group.

I called Jon again. "Hey, tell me about the training group you joined when you got started."

"I signed up for an Ironman class at UW-Sports Med," he told me.

"Are they all fast?" I said.

"Yeah, they're all pretty good. But I really think you can handle it. There's two groups—one for beginners and one for competitive Ironman triathletes. You should definitely sign up for the competitive group."

"I just don't want to get in over my head," I said.

"You'll fit in," he said. "Don't worry."

When I called the facility to inquire about the class, I was told that there was still room in the competitive Ironman class and I signed up on the spot.

Despite what Jon had told me, I was still wary about how I would fit in with this group, as most of them were Ironman veterans. My longest race to this point was an Olympic-distance event, and I had never even run a marathon. The class met twice each week, on Wednesday night and Saturday morning, and I was anxious to get started. My first workout, a run-spin session, was scheduled for a Wednesday evening during the second week of October.

The week before the training class started, Lisa decided to go on an unusual diet that was supposed to last for 10 days and required her to drink nothing but organic lemon juice mixed with maple syrup, cayenne pepper, and distilled water along with an herbal laxative tea morning and night. This diet was supposed to cleanse the body of toxins and clean out the digestive tract. Along with all solid food, caffeine and alcohol were prohibited. In order to provide some moral support, I decided to try the diet with her, thinking that it would provide enough calories to meet my needs throughout my daily schedule, including workouts. I started on Monday morning, knowing that my first group workout was scheduled for Wednesday evening. I renounced my morning cup of coffee and mixed up a couple of batches of lemonade, and we started cleansing.

I made it through the entire day Tuesday, but on Wednesday morning I woke up with a pounding headache. I assumed it was my body's reaction to going another day without a healthy dose of caffeine. I managed to slog through the day, and late Wednesday afternoon I packed my bag and headed to UW Sports Med for my first group run. Jon had introduced me to a couple of the people in the group at some informal summer workouts, but I didn't know much about any of them. I was nervous that I was in over my head, thinking maybe I should have started in the beginners' class, but decided to give it the old college try.

"Have fun!" Lisa called as I left the house. I detected a hint of skepticism in her voice, but I was just happy to be heading off to an organized practice again.

Ten people showed up for our initial workout, and we started out for a 50-minute run that consisted of a 20-minute warm-up followed by some interval work and a 10-minute cool-down. We returned to the facility and changed into our biking gear to get ready for a spin workout that was scheduled to last for 80 minutes. As the new guy in the class, I wanted to make an impression on the regulars in the group.

I was unfamiliar with the rigors of indoor spinning, and I hammered away as hard as I could from the outset of the session. The first 20 minutes went fine, and then suddenly I felt something strange happening to my body. I started getting light-headed and sweating profusely, even more than normal. My stomach felt queasy and in need of food at the same time, and I noticed that my peripheral vision began to gradually fade away until it seemed as though I was looking through a couple of paper towel tubes.

I wasn't quite sure what was happening, but it didn't feel very good. My competitive instincts kicked in and I tried to push through the discomfort, regain my composure, and finish the workout. I noticed that the spin teacher kept glancing at me from the front of the room with a concerned look on his face. I finally started to slow down because I simply could not keep my legs spinning any longer. My head drooped, and I felt as though I was going to fall off the bike and land in a crumpled heap on the floor.

The instructor got off his bike and came to the back of the room. "Are you feeling all right?" he asked.

All I said was, "I need food!" I stopped pedaling, unclipped my shoes, dismounted, and stood there with my hands on my knees, sweat dripping into a puddle on the floor in front of me. I had neglected to bring anything to eat and drink, so John Hollenhorst, who was spinning next to me, got off his bike and ran to the locker room. He returned with two power bars, a banana, and a bottle of Gatorade. I wolfed down both power bars, guzzled half the bottle of Gatorade, gobbled down the banana, and finished the drink.

"You bonked," the instructor said.

"Yeah, I guess I did," I answered. I had heard the term "bonking" before but had no idea what caused it, what it felt like, or how to prevent it. I suspect that my lemonade diet had not provided quite enough energy to sustain my body through an arduous workout, and I decided to let Lisa finish cleansing by herself. After there was some food in my system, I miraculously began to perk up. I was able to regain my strength and finish the spin workout.

When I got home Lisa said, "How did your first practice go?"

"I bonked," I admitted. "But I finished the workout."

"Of course you did," she said. "I'm sure you'd finish the workout if you had two broken legs and brain damage."

"I'd sure try," I said accepting her compliment.

On Saturday morning I headed to the second workout, a swim-spin session that began at 8 o'clock. Besides my clothing and shoes, I took a big selection of food this time, including cherry crunch Harvest Bars, Gatorade, bananas, apples, and oatmeal raisin cookies. I think I had enough to feed the entire group and their families.

Our coach wrote the workout schedule on a marker board at the end of the pool, and I jumped into lane 3 and started the 300-yard warm-up. The other swimmers in lane 3 passed me a couple of times before we had gone 100 yards. A couple of times one of them stopped halfway down the lane and turned around to avoid having to climb over me again. I got the distinct feeling that they were irritated with me and that I had committed some sort of gaffe in swimming pool etiquette. After we finished our warm-up, the instructor came over. He said, "Dan, why don't you come over to lane 1 for the main set."

"Sure," I said, thinking that I had been promoted. It wasn't long before I realized, however, that I had actually been demoted to the slow lane with swimmers who were more my speed. The rest of the workout went smoothly and I began to feel more comfortable with my fellow competitors.

Our training group was composed of a diverse group of people, male and female, ranging in age from 23 to 57. The youngest member of the group, a 23-year-old medical student, happened to be the daughter of the oldest man in the group, a 57-year-old business executive. Other group members included a lawyer, the CEO of a software company, a dermatologist, a marketing VP, a general manager of a publishing company, a nurse, an engineer, an aerobics instructor, and myself, a retired middle-school teacher and coach. Our instructor and coach was a 26-year-old professional triathlete from New Zealand named Will Smith who lived in the Madison area and worked part-time at the sports clinic to help make ends meet. He never missed a session, participating in most of them even though he was much faster than all of us, and kept all the workouts focused but fun.

It was obvious to me from the start that I was one of the slower swimmers and runners in the group, but I took some solace from the fact that I was strong on the bike. The weekly training sessions became more and more comfortable, and I began to look forward to each workout. I tried to train six days a week with one day off, and as the months rolled past, my fitness base solidified and I steadily rounded into better and better condition.

I scheduled a race for early April, 2004, in Las Vegas. Lisa had a business event there, and I wanted to experience what it was like to travel with my bike and race out of town. I rented a travel case and asked one of the mechanics at the bike shop to teach me how to disassemble the bike. I watched intently as he broke the bike down and carefully packed it away. I didn't think I'd have any trouble taking my bike apart; putting it back together would be a different story.

I shipped the bike out to our hotel, and it was there waiting for me when we arrived. It took me a while, but I somehow managed to reassemble it with no parts left over. I took it out for an hour ride into the hills outside the city, and everything seemed to be in working order. A buddy of mine from Vegas agreed to pick me up on the morning of the race, and he was as good as his word. The front desk gave me a wake-up call at 4:30 A.M., telling me that there was somebody waiting for me in the lobby. It was pitch-black outside as we drove 40 minutes from downtown Las Vegas to Lake Meade.

This was the first time this event had been run. When we got to the race site, the people in charge were still setting up tents and bike racks and getting the transition area organized. After I unloaded my stuff we pitched in and helped the organizers get things ready. I had heard that the water in Lake Meade was pretty cold in the spring, but I had been so busy I didn't even think about that until after I had my wet suit on.

I waded into the water to feel the temperature and discovered that it was colder than I could have even imagined. My wet suit was short sleeved, and I noticed that just about everybody else was wearing a long-sleeved suit. Many of the other racers were also wearing full wet suit caps. I went back to the transition area, removed the top of my wet suit, and pulled on a tight, long-sleeved body armor shirt that I had brought with me thinking that it would help keep me warm during the swim. I took my watch off and buckled it over the top of my left sleeve so that I could see it better once the race started. As usual, I had butterflies before the race started and was worried that the cold water would make it difficult to swim.

Five minutes before my wave was scheduled to start, I entered the water and tried to warm up. The water didn't seem to be any warmer than an hour before, and I hoped that once I started swimming I would adjust to it. As soon as the horn sounded, I took the plunge and struck out for the first buoy. I immediately started hyperventilating. For the first time I panicked as the frigid water took my breath away and the tight shirt fatigued my shoulders. After two minutes of swimming, I stopped to tread water in an effort to catch my breath. The shoreline was 200 yards away, and I was sorely tempted to turn and head in that direction, get out of the water, and abandon the race. In the end, though, I decided to continue.

I rolled onto my back, told myself to relax, and tried to get my breathing under control. After a minute I turned over again, continued the swim, and finally started to warm up a bit. It was the worst swim I had ever experienced, and when I neared the end and started walking up the beach ramp I fell down. I got up but stumbled again. This time another racer stopped, grabbed my arm, and helped me to my feet.

When I reached my bike I peeled off the wet suit with a pair of numb hands and then made the mistake of trying to take off my shirt. I pulled it over my head and peeled the right sleeve off. When I tried to pull off the left sleeve, it dawned on me that I had put my watch over it. I couldn't pull the shirt out from underneath the watch, so I had to quickly untangle the shirt, put it back on, and continue.

My feet were numb as I started the bike. They didn't thaw out until halfway through the ride. As the sun came up over the mountains, I gradually began to warm up. By the time I got off the bike I felt inspired by the beautiful vista and uplifted by the energy in the group.

For the first time in a race, nobody passed me on the run. Maybe this was because I was so far back in the pack after the lousy swim that there was nobody left to pass me, but I took it as a good sign. In fact, I chased down a couple of slower runners and passed them. As I went past one guy, I said "Hey, you're the first runner I've ever passed in a race!"

He looked at me and said, "Thanks for that positive bit of news."

My results in this race were less than admirable, but as with each previous race, I learned from the mistakes I made.

One of the physical and mental hurdles that I knew I had to get over before doing an Ironman was to run a marathon. My plan was to run in the Mad-City Marathon in Madison in late May before resuming my triathlon race schedule. My buddy Kevin also had the marathon on his schedule. He had already run marathons in Milwaukee and Chicago, so he had some valuable experience that put him a few steps ahead of me. He and his family stayed at our place the day before the race, and that afternoon we drove part of the course and secreted a couple of bottles of energy drink along the route.

On the morning of the race we headed downtown to pick up our packets. When I got to the table, the volunteer who was working there couldn't find my name. I wanted to blame the organizers for poor management, but suddenly I had a vague feeling that it was my fault. I thought I had registered online four months earlier, but apparently thinking about it was as far as I had gotten. My name was not on the list, and same-day registration for the marathon was not allowed. Kevin saw me standing there with a dumb look on my face and started laughing.

"What's the matter, did you forget to register?" he said.

"Apparently," I said

"You're an idiot," he said.

"Thanks, man," I said.

Luckily there were three other distances being run that day, so I switched lines and signed up for the 5K race and then just ran the marathon instead. The weather was cloudy and cool—perfect running conditions. Those perfect conditions, unfortunately, began to deteriorate around mile 6. About an hour into the run it started to sprinkle, then stopped for a bit. Then rain started to come down hard and never let up the rest of the way. We sloshed through 20 miles of puddles, soaked from head to toe. This actually turned out to be good for hydration, but running with wet shoes and socks for three hours was not enjoyable.

Kevin and I stuck together for the first half of the race. At one point he said, "My shoes are so heavy, I feel like Herman Munster." I was determined to run my own race at my own pace, and gradually I crept ahead of him. At mile 18 I started up the hill that leads into the University of Wisconsin Arboretum and saw Lisa and Nancy standing under big umbrellas trying to keep dry. I think both of them expected to see Kevin first, and as I passed them they looked at each other with somewhat puzzled expressions on their faces. "He's back there somewhere," I told them. "I don't know how far."

I had heard people talk of hitting the wall after 20 miles in a marathon, but at that point in the race I still felt pretty good. My wall didn't appear until mile 24. By that time my legs and hips had had just about enough. I stopped to walk for a bit until a guy I knew passed me and offered a word of encouragement. I started running slowly again, knowing that the finish line was approaching. As I came abreast of another runner, she said "Hi."

I said, "Am I even moving?"

"You're doing great. We're almost home."

I was greatly relieved to pass under the finishing clock, pick up my medal, and get out of the rain. Officially, I ran a 4:05 5K, which would have undoubtedly been the slowest 5K time in the history of the world. But I knew now that I could handle a marathon.

At this point I had roughly three months to get ready for Ironman and was looking forward to an increased workout schedule. Even though our group training had officially ended at the end of May, we did get together for regular summer workouts. We met Monday and Friday mornings for open water swims, Tuesday and Thursday afternoons for bike rides, and Wednesday mornings for speed work. We did occasional long bricks on Saturdays and long runs on Sundays. Everybody worked hard, and I felt more and more confident that I could complete Ironman in a respectable time, ideally 12 hours or less.

I spent June, July, and August training, racing, and anticipating the big day that was to come in early September. We invited a couple of friends from New Mexico to stay with us the week of the Ironman. Both had done nine previous Ironman races and I hoped that their experience would be a benefit to me. On our part, Lisa and I would provide them with free, comfortable lodging, good food, and good company. The week of Ironman finally arrived. I was nervous, excited, and determined to . . .

Chapter 7
Enjoy the Ironman Experience

Having Ironman Veterans Stay With You
the Week of the Race Can Wear You Out

Glenn McCarrol and Danny Montoya, my two friends from Las Cruces, New Mexico, arrived separately the week of the race. Glenn and his wife Kelly flew in on Tuesday afternoon and I picked them up at the airport. We had met on a business trip six months earlier and after sharing some triathlon stories had discovered that we were both registered for Ironman Wisconsin. Glenn was an intimidating specimen—a chiseled, muscular triathlete who had been an All-American age-grouper before burning out on the sport at age 40.

After two years away, he had decided to get back into competition, and now at the age of 44 was gradually working himself back into racing shape. He had competed in Ironman Brazil four months earlier and run a respectable time of 10:50:02. I plied him with questions all the way to our place. "How much do you think we should train this week?" "Do you want to preview the entire bike course?" "Do you think we should swim every morning?" "What do you like to eat?" "How much sleep do you need at night?" He was amused at my wide-eyed excitement and nicknamed me "Rookie."

On Wednesday morning Glenn and I got up at 6 o'clock and headed to the swim site. The official Gatorade morning swims were not scheduled to start until the next day, but Glenn wanted to get in the water and swim an easy mile. The swim site was located on the west side of Lake

Monona in the shadow of the Frank Lloyd Wright-designed Monona Terrace Community and Convention Center, which had been built right on the shoreline. It was a beautiful morning. Quite a few early-morning swimmers were already in the water and more were on the shore tugging on wet suits. The 77-degree water felt very warm as we waded into the lake, and I was concerned about overheating in a long-sleeved wet suit.

We swam for 40 minutes along the shoreline, stopped a couple of times to talk, and enjoyed the view of the sun coming up over the eastern shore of the lake. I felt pretty good even though I had no hope of keeping up with Glenn in the water. I received a small confidence boost when both of us swam by a group of 10 or 12 other swimmers who had started before us. I frequently had to remind myself that there were always going to be people faster than me and there were always going to be people slower than me. I had resigned myself to the fact that I was a mid-pack swimmer but countered that reality with the thought that the swim was the least important leg of Ironman and that I could always make up time on the bike.

We exited the water after a moderately hard workout and walked back to the car. Glenn had raced all over the world and recognized quite a few of the other competitors that were there. He had nicknames for some of them. "Hey, it's Business Dude and Business Chick," he said as a middle-aged couple walked past us toward the water.

"Who are they?" I asked.

"I saw them in Brazil in May. The guy always had a suit on when he wasn't training and the woman was always dressed up too. Business Dude is fast, bro. I think he's one of the guys sponsored by Timex."

On the way home we stopped at a bike shop so Glenn could get a part he needed for his bike. He had been having trouble with his aero position and wanted to tinker with it before Sunday. That afternoon, after he made some adjustments on his bike, we headed out for a one-loop ride on the Ironman bike course.

The bike course at Ironman Wisconsin is a two-loop route that starts in downtown Madison, heads out into some rolling rural countryside, and cuts through the towns of Verona, Mt. Horeb, and Cross Plains. It's a beautiful yet challenging ride. There aren't any long stretches where you can settle down into your aerobars and hammer away. Instead, there are lots of small rolling hills and a handful of short steep hills that make even the best riders work pretty hard. During my months of training, I had ridden the course at least 20 times and knew every part of it like the back of my hand.

Glenn and I rode at a vigorous pace, and I talked about the course as we rode. I told him where there was a stretch of freshly laid pea gravel, where the tough hills were, where I had seen dogs in the past, and where the aid stations would be set up. I kept pace with him quite easily but had the feeling that he could leave me in the dust any time he chose. The route from my house to the loop and back was exactly 56 miles. We arrived back home in slightly under three hours, cleaned up our bikes, and got a bite to eat.

On Thursday morning Glenn and I got up early again and headed back to the lake for another swim. As we got close to the lake, we were happy to see that the buoys used to mark the swim course were in place. A giant green Gatorade bottle was inflated and anchored on the shore near the water.

As we got there, around 7:30, the place was already crawling with people. The folks from Gatorade had a set up an area where competitors could check their bags for safekeeping while they swam. U2's "Beautiful Day" was blasting at full volume out of two huge speakers. At a booth full of Ironman wet suits that were available for test swims, a rep was helping a tall woman into a suit while explaining the correct way to pull it on. I could feel a buzz of energy emanating from the scene. We did one loop of the swim course—Glenn exited the water in 30 minutes, and I followed him out nine minutes later.

We immediately changed into running gear and ran the first 5 miles of the run course. The run starts at the Convention Center, heads up Martin Luther King Boulevard, turns down State Street, and then veers off on a fairly tight route that winds through downtown Madison and the campus of the University of Wisconsin. Like the bike course, it consists of two loops, and it has a cruel twist to it as the runners must turn around for the start of the second loop less than 100 yards from the finish line. This morning's run seemed like an easy one, but I had an ominous sense that I wouldn't feel quite as spry when I did it after a 112-mile bike ride.

Danny was scheduled to get into Madison on Thursday afternoon. After lunch Glenn and I headed to the airport to pick him up. When we pulled up at the terminal Danny was waiting curbside with his bike box and bags. Glenn gave him a hug and introduced him to me. He and Glenn live in the same city and had met years before at a race.

Danny was 31 years old, stood about 5' 9", and weighed 135 pounds. He had lean, angular features and clean-shaven, muscular legs— identifying characteristics of many triathletes. He worked as the manager of the natatorium at New Mexico State University and was an experienced Ironman veteran. When I asked him if he wanted to swim or ride or run, he didn't seem too concerned about doing any of them. "I'm ready, dude," was all he said.

Before taking Danny back to my place, we stopped by the Convention Center to register, pick up our race packets, and do a little shopping at the Ironman Expo. We waited 30 minutes in line to register, and when Danny came out of the room he was smiling from ear to ear. "Paula Newby-Frasier checked me in, bro!" She was his favorite, I learned, yet I don't think I would have recognized her. As we walked through the changing areas scouting things out I said, "You know, one of the things I like best about triathlon is the fact that everybody is so friendly."

"Yeah," Glenn agreed, "it's like a close-knit family."

Just then an older guy walked into the changing room, tripped over the rolled-up end of some temporary carpeting, and fell down. Glenn quickly bent over and offered to help him to his feet, but the guy angrily slapped Glenn's hand away. He got up muttering, "What stupid idiot put that carpet there? I'm going to find out and tell somebody off!"

We looked at each other and then started laughing. "There goes your theory, bro," Danny said.

"I don't think Angry Carpet Guy quite fits your profile of the friendly triathlete," Glenn told me.

We made a swing through the crowded expo. Glenn and Danny called each other "Rockefeller" as they made purchases for friends back home. I was hesitant to buy anything since I thought it was wrong to wear Ironman gear before actually finishing the race. I finally found a couple of shirts, a cap, and a coffee cup, and we headed home.

On Friday morning Glenn wanted to swim again, but neither Danny nor I felt like it. I was worried that I had done too much over the past couple of days, but we drove down to the lake again and hung around while Glenn did a third practice loop. Danny pointed to a couple standing on the shoreline. "Dude, it's Tattoo Man and Tattoo Woman." I had seen this pair before at races and apparently so had Danny. Both were covered with bizarre-looking tattoos from head to toe.

"I've seen them around at a couple of races near Madison. Strangest-looking pair I've ever seen, bro," I said.

After Glenn finished his swim we made one final trip to the bike shop located near the swim start to have somebody help him with his aerobars. I picked up a new water cage, as one of mine had broken the day before, and then we decided to bike the first 16 miles of the Ironman loop just to show Danny a portion of the course. We rode the first 16 miles and then looped back into town a different way, making it a leisurely 30-mile ride. Friday afternoon we finally got off our feet. We sat around and did nothing before heading out to a restaurant for dinner and then off to my son's high school football game.

On Saturday morning we did nothing strenuous. We spent part of the morning organizing our gear and checking our bikes one last time. Danny, Glenn, and I lined up all of our colored bags and started packing food and clothes and all the things that we would need. We stuck reflective tape on our shoes and shirts and put our race numbers on our bikes and helmets.

From that first race two years ago to my first Ironman, I had learned to make do with less and had pared my packing list down to about 38 items. After lunch on Saturday we loaded our bikes and gear into the car and drove back to the Convention Center. We dropped our bikes off at the transition area and put our bags in the changing rooms. As we walked away from the transition area we ran into a guy that Danny knew from New Mexico. "Hey, Scott, what brings you here?" Danny said.

"I'm doing Ironman," he said.

"I didn't know you were racing, bro," said Danny. "How many races have you done?"

"This is my first," he said.

"Your first Ironman?"

"My first race," he said again. "My brother and I made a bet last year when we were out partying one night. I told him that I could do an Ironman if I really wanted to."

"Where have you been training?" Danny asked him.

"I've been working out with a group from Albuquerque."

"Have you done much open water swimming?" I asked him.

"No," he said. "This will be my first time swimming in a lake."

Glenn, Danny, and I looked at each other. "Well, good luck, bro," Glenn said.

"What's his last name?" I asked.

"I don't know," Danny said.

I made a mental note to remember his first name and city he was from so that I could check the results when it was over. I had my doubts about his finishing and could already picture "DNF" after his name.

The pre-race meeting was held in the large first-floor convention hall. We walked in just as it was getting started, and I was surprised to see that the room was packed. We had to look around for a while to find a table with three empty chairs. "Do you guys always go to the pre-race meetings?" I asked them.

"Of course," Glenn said. "It's part of the routine."

There was a panel of pros sitting on a stage up front, including the previous year's winner, Dave Harju, and a bunch of the other racers from the team sponsored by Timex. We listened to the question-and-answer session in which first-timers had a chance to ask about nutrition, strategy, and the like.

We were given an overview of the rules by Charlie Crawford, the longtime head official from Ironman North America. He talked in great detail about drafting rules on the bike and then regaled us with some of the more obscure rules that govern the sport. My favorite was the rule that states, "Crawling is not allowed on the run course." I hoped I wouldn't have to test that ruling on Sunday afternoon.

Finally we were introduced to three of the men who had competed in the very first Ironman more than 25 years ago. Two of them were competing again and looked as though they were still in excellent shape. The oldest competitor, a 75-year-old named Frank Farrar, was recognized. After receiving a final wish for a successful race, we were dismissed.

On the way home we talked about our time goals. Danny had a personal best of 9:59 and was hoping to run as close to 10 hours as possible. Glenn had trained sporadically, and at 10 pounds over his normal race weight he didn't know if he would be able to break 11 hours. My time goals had been carefully formed and were etched in my mind. I wanted to be in the water for 75 minutes, finish the bike in six hours, and run the marathon in 4:30, with 16 minutes allotted for transition times. I hoped to cross the finish line at 7:00 P.M. if everything went according to plan. "Nothing ever goes according to plan in an Ironman," Glenn reminded me.

"Something will always surprise you," Danny added. "Sometimes the surprises will be good; sometimes they'll be bad. But you can always count on something unexpected happening out there."

"I think I'm quite clear on that point," I said.

Saturday night we had spaghetti for dinner and spent the evening talking and relaxing and thinking about the day to come.

Late Saturday night we still had a houseful of guests. Everybody was wired even though we all knew it would be a short night. Glenn and Danny called it quits around 11:00 and I followed shortly afterward. Somewhat strangely, I didn't have much trouble getting to sleep even though I was wound up and knew I would be waking up in a few short hours. I didn't hear Lisa come to bed an hour later, and I didn't remember dreaming about anything that night. I guess I had resigned myself to my fate. I had been faithful in my training, had a pretty good nutrition plan, and felt as though I was in control of all the aspects of the race that could be controlled. I realized that there was nothing left for me to do except . . .

Chapter 8
Get Some Sleep, Get Up Early, and Race 140.6 Miles

I'm Nervous, But Apparently Not As Nervous As the Woman Throwing Up in the Porta-Potty Next to Me

I had set the alarm for 4:00 A.M., but I woke up with a start at 3:15, rolled over, and looked at Lisa. She was lying next to me on her back, straight and still, with her arms at her side and her eyes wide open. I poked her gently in the side and whispered, "Honey, are you awake?"

"Yes, I haven't been able to sleep at all. I was trying to lie still so I wouldn't wake you up. I'm so nervous I think I have diarrhea." Having said that, she rolled out of bed and bolted for the bathroom. I got up, slipped on some shorts, and walked downstairs. It was tranquil outside and pitch-black. After nearly two years of training, planning, and anticipating, the big day had finally arrived.

I had developed a pre-race routine that I intended to follow the morning of Ironman. Everybody that I talked to told me the same thing, "Don't change anything that you've been doing during your training." I started getting breakfast ready and soon heard Glenn and Danny coming up from the basement to the kitchen. They both looked refreshed considering that they had slept only five hours.

"How ya feelin', bro?" Danny asked me. "You look calm, man. I don't ever think I've seen anybody so relaxed before their first Ironman."

"Dude, I'm nervous on the inside," I said. Glenn and Danny had called each other "bro" and "dude" all week, and I had picked up on the habit as well. "I actually feel like throwing up." They both laughed. I cooked up a pan of oatmeal, sliced some strawberries, and toasted some bagels. We sat down to a hearty breakfast at 4:45, two hours and 15 minutes before the start of the race.

It didn't register when I first got downstairs, but when I looked around I saw that there were small paper signs taped all over the kitchen. Apparently the kids had been busy after the three of us had gone to bed at 11 o'clock. "Glenn, the bike is your favorite!" one sign said. Another said "Dan, I can't wait to hug you at the finish line even though you'll be sweating like a pig!" There was one that said, "You guys will kick butt today!" I set the automatic timer on my camera and took a couple of pictures of the three of us eating breakfast. I didn't feel very hungry but I knew I had to eat a lot, so I forced down a big bowl of oatmeal and strawberries topped with organic brown sugar and milk, plus a banana, and drank a cup of coffee and a bottle of Gatorade.

All week long we had been watching the forecast and had hoped for a day with temperatures in the low 70s. The thermometer outside the screened-in porch already registered 67 degrees, which meant that the forecasters were undoubtedly going to be wrong. It was going to be a lot warmer than everybody expected, and that was not good news. I thought back to last year when temperatures had risen into the low 90s and precipitated an inordinate number of DNFs, and already I began to worry about hydration problems that I might encounter. After eating, we stacked our dishes in the sink, packed up the things that had not already been dropped off at the race site, and got ready to leave.

"Are you guys nervous?" I asked as we drove downtown.

"Sure, bro," said Danny. "I remember my first Ironman. I was so nervous that I got sick before it started."

"I just hope I don't get pummeled at the start of the swim and that I don't have any flat tires," I said.

"You'll be fine, dude," said Glenn. "You've put in your time training. You're in good shape. You're going to have a great race. I felt the same way before my first Ironman," he said. "Everything worked out great."

I appreciated his optimism, but it didn't quell the butterflies I had fluttering around in my stomach. I had always gotten nervous before athletic events in high school and college.

During my first year of college football, the players on our team all had different ways of dealing with nerves. Some threw up. Some walked nervously around the locker room occasionally screaming and punching things. Some listened to music. I dealt with nerves by falling asleep. After suiting up I would put my helmet on, put my mouth guard in, and take a short snooze.

Before my first game as a freshman I made the mistake of falling asleep on one of the benches right in the middle of the locker room. A couple of seniors carefully taped my helmet and my feet to the bench and then yelled "All right, let's GO!" I jerked awake thinking the team was about to take the field and was surprised to discover that I couldn't lift my head or feet. After that I always found a quiet, out-of-the-way corner to take my pre-game nap. The one thing that almost all the players had in common was the customary pre-game dump. In our home locker room, accommodating 40 players was never a problem because there were plenty of stalls. On the road it was always a different story.

One school we played was renovating the locker rooms, and we were relegated to a small temporary construction trailer. When it was time for our traditional pre-game routine, we discovered that there was only one toilet. After further examination of that single fixture, we found out that not only did the toilet not work, it wasn't even hooked up to anything. As unattractive as it now seems, the only choice was for all of us to use that solitary porcelain receptacle, and a few players exited the stall looking less composed than when they had entered.

As we approached the Capitol Square it was eerie to see how bright and busy it was. Temporary lights had been set up around the Square to illuminate the transition and bag drop areas. Ordinarily on a Sunday morning the Square would be deserted and quiet. Today it was a beehive of activity. Cars topped with bike carriers were parked everywhere; others crept along looking for that elusive empty parking spot. Down every street that radiated from the staging area, competitors were solemnly walking. They all carried their special needs bags toward the drop area and then converged on Martin Luther King Boulevard, the street that fed directly into the transition area atop the Convention Center. The closest parking spot I could find was five blocks away. We shouldered our backpacks and started walking toward the transition area.

After we dropped our bags off near the Capitol we continued toward the parking lot where all the bikes were parked. I could hear music pumping out of the speakers that were set up somewhere down the block. I happened across a couple of my training buddies from Madison. "Good luck today," I told each of them. "Hope to see you out on the course."

51

"You too, Dan. Have a great time!"

It started to get crowded as we got closer to the transition area. The announcer kept repeating, "Please make sure you get down to the water in plenty of time. The transition area will close at 6:30 sharp!" It was 5:45 and we still had a lot to do. We walked into the Convention Center and cruised through both changing areas to see that our bags were in the right places. From there we proceeded to the bike transition area to make sure our tires were inflated, water bottles were filled, and chains were oiled.

The body marking area was packed, and it was difficult to see where the lines began and ended. I got in line behind a group of anxious racers and watched as each person ahead of me was tagged with black magic marker—left arm, left thigh, and right calf. I saw that the girl marking people in my line was writing really small numbers on everybody, so I jumped lines when I noticed that the guy next to her was marking in big, bold numbers. The announcer kept repeating his plea for people to hustle down to the swim start, and it didn't seem possible that everybody could get marked and down there in time.

I met up with Glenn and Danny again and we all made one final stop at the line of porta-potties. Then we pulled on our wet suits and made our way to the swim start. The transition area at Ironman Wisconsin is different from any other I've seen. The swim-to-bike transition requires that everybody run a couple hundred yards up one of the two helixes that bookend the Convention Center's parking ramp. As we left the building I felt like an animal being led to slaughter. We were herded down the spiral ramp, all the while being goaded by the announcer's warning that the transition area would be closing soon.

The entrance to the water at this race is very narrow—10 yards at most—and the crowd of racers bottlenecked at the green carpeted ramp that had been set up for entering and exiting the water. I was still very nervous. I kept shifting my weight from foot to foot and wondering where Glenn and Danny were, since we had been separated in the crowd. Suddenly I heard somebody yelling, "There he is! Hey, Dan!" I turned and saw that Lisa and our three kids had wormed their way through the crowd at the starting line. They were waving excitedly as I slowly moved toward the water. The day before, Lisa had asked, "How am I going to be able to tell which one you are in the water?"

I said, "I'll be the one in the black wet suit with the purple swim cap."

"Oh, OK," she said before the silliness of my answer became clear. "Very funny, dude," she said. She had picked up the speech habits of the moment.

From talking to people who had competed in this event before, I was prepared for the fact that I would be in the lake treading water for 15 to 20 minutes before the race began. I finally reached the ramp that sloped into the water. Before taking the step that would mark the point of no return, I looked back one more time and waved to Lisa. "Good luck," she mouthed. "I love you."

I slid quietly into the water and meandered through the crowd of swimmers bobbing up and down. It was a 200-yard swim from the shore to the starting line, and I slowly made my way to the far side of the starting area. Colored flags had been set up behind the starting line for swimmers to seed themselves. My goal was to complete the swim in 1:15, so I floated toward the third colored flag and tried to find some space to tread water. I was still nervous, but the energy I had to expend floating helped calm my nerves. I checked my watch and saw that it was 6:50. "First Ironman?" I asked the guy next to me.

"Yeah. Yours?"

"Yup," I said. "I can't wait to get started." I looked back toward the shore and noticed that there was still a long line of people who had not yet entered the water. "I wonder if they'll start on time if everybody isn't in the water."

"I think they try to start right at 7:00," the guy said.

"They have the green flag flying," I said. "Better get ready. They could fire the cannon any—"

BOOM! Before I could finish the sentence, the starting gun went off and the mass of swimmers started churning toward the flags hanging over the starting line. The abruptness of the start caught me by surprise. I quickly turned around, clicked my stopwatch, kicked forward, and tried to find a small piece of open water. Off to my left the sun was coming up over the trees on the east edge of the lake. The orange glow colored the sky and the water, giving the whole scene a feeling of warmth. The last thing I saw before I started swimming was a large group of swimmers still trying to get into the water as the gun sounded. Then I was off.

The first 50 yards were crowded as everybody tried to get clear of the swimmers close by. I got bumped a few times on both sides but never got kicked. My plan was to start right next to the first large corner buoy and then swim inside the smaller markers to each corner. After about 100 yards of choppy swimming I finally found a little space even though I was sandwiched between two other people who were swimming at the same speed as I was. I knew I was in the right spot as nobody crawled over me to pass, and the woman to my left was pacing me perfectly. I stayed with her for 400 yards, and every time I breathed and looked I saw her in the exact same stroke position. It was like swimming under a strobe light.

I had watched the first two Ironman Wisconsin starts from the top of the Convention Center, and from that vantage point it didn't look as though there was room for anybody to swim. The effect was that of a massive school of fish churning the lake into a frothy maelstrom. In the water, however, it was a different story. Once I found some space to swim I didn't get bumped until the first turn buoy.

I usually breathe to my left, but during the first leg of the first loop I forced myself to breath to the right in order to get a look at the shoreline. It was incredible to see thousands of spectators lining the top and sides of the Convention Center and standing along the shore for half a mile in both directions. I couldn't hear any sounds except the steady swoosh of the water flowing past my ears and the slap of swimmers' arms hitting the water.

When I got to the first corner, I slowed to make the turn and ran into some congestion as many of the swimmers had stopped to sight the next buoy. Somebody yelled, "Come on, everybody, you gotta keep moving!" I slipped under the right corner of the buoy, and as I straightened out I got kicked hard on the right side of my head and the seal on my goggles was compromised. I had to stop and refit the mask to my face before continuing. I surged forward again, made the second turn, and started down the backstretch of the first loop. I stayed inside the line of buoys and now had nobody flanking me on either side. As I finished the first lap, I checked my watch. I was pleased to see that I had gotten back to the start in 37 minutes, which was two minutes quicker than the fastest practice lap I had timed. I didn't feel as though I had been pushing that hard, so I set my sights on trying to finish the swim under 1:15.

The second loop was as uneventful as the first. I felt like I had a good rhythm going and was hopeful of beating my swim goal. As I finished the second lap I sighted on the giant Gatorade bottle, put my head back in the water, and headed for shore. I was in the middle of a large group of swimmers as I pulled for the green exit ramp, and we all seemed infused with energy as the end of the swim loomed close at hand. With 50 yards to go I tried to finish as fast as I could, and after 20 strokes I finally felt the carpeted ramp with my right hand.

I stumbled as I walked up the ramp. I felt disoriented, as I almost always did after going from completely horizontal in the water to an upright position. I pulled off the goggles and swim cap, unzipped my wet suit, and pulled my arms free as I ran to the bottom of the helix that was manned with helpers whose only job it was to strip wet suits off the tired swimmers. The lap timer on my watch was already running past 1:20, so my second loop had not been as fast as I had hoped.

I had planned to take the wet suit off in the changing room to avoid being dragged across the carpet on my back. I had a change of heart when a tall, good-natured helper called out "Hey, over here! I'll help you with your wet suit. Just lie down on your back." Without thinking, I dropped onto my back and put my feet up to meet his hands, and he jerked off the wet suit cleanly in two seconds. He handed it to me as I got up, and I folded it across my arm as I started running up the circular drive to the top of the building and the swim-to-bike changing room. I felt a little self-conscious in my red and black Speedo, but nobody seemed to notice me in the midst of hundreds of other Speedo-clad men and women.

The volunteers in the swim-to-bike area were extremely friendly and helpful. I grabbed my bag of clothes and looked for an open bench to sit on while changing. Since there were no women in the men's area we could strip down to our birthday suits without offending anybody. In all of my previous races I had worn a tri-suit and just changed shoes. I was worried about being comfortable on the bike for six hours that day, so I decided to wear regular biking gear on the ride and then change again before the run. I got my bibs on without any difficulty, but my jersey got tangled up around my neck and I needed help getting it pulled down over my shoulders and back.

I had heard that racers thought it was a good idea to put Vaseline on their nipples before the run to prevent chafing, but in my hurry to untangle the bike jersey, I forgot. Luckily chafing didn't become a problem. It's not easy putting clothes on when you're wet and sweaty and in a hurry, and I knew my transition time was going to be terrible. I had allotted eight minutes for each transition, and as I headed out the door, running carefully in the biking shoes, my watch passed 10 minutes. "Where do you want sunscreen?" a young woman asked as I came out the door.

"Everywhere!" I said.

"Stand still, I'll get you." She quickly slathered my face, neck, arms, and legs with sunscreen and I ran toward the bike transition area ready to ride.

The bikes were all racked in the top parking area of the Convention Center, a hundred yards long. As I ran between the rows of bike racks I saw a volunteer standing with my bike ready to roll. I took it from him and said "Thanks, buddy." I hopped on at the end of the parking area and wound my way carefully down the helix at the opposite end of the building from the swim site. Some of the racers had walked their bikes all the way down the spiral and were mounting at the bottom, causing a bit of a roadblock as I came around the corner. I saw a friend just heading out. "How did your swim go?" I asked him.

"Just about what I expected," he said. "1:19. See you out on the course."

My plan was to try to hold back a bit for the first two hours of the ride. Our coach had warned us about trashing ourselves early on the bike. It was hard to suppress all the energy I had, however, and I decided to go hard and try to pass some of the people who were apparently better swimmers than me. One guy jokingly said "Crappy swimmer!" as I passed him. I carried two water bottles and a spare tubular with me, knowing that there would be plenty of food at the aid stations. My plan was to drink half a bottle of Gatorade right after getting on the bike and then to eat or drink something every 15 minutes the rest of the day. The temperature was still mid-morning cool, the sky was cloudless, and there was a warm south wind starting to blow. This turned out to be an ominous harbinger of things to come.

The bike course was very crowded from the time I started, and it was difficult to stay clear of other riders. I had taken Charlie Crawford at his word during the pre-race rules meeting and was worried about getting penalized for drafting. Every time I heard a motorcycle behind me I was fearful that the official was watching me, so I made sure that I stayed clear of other riders.

In a previous race that summer I had been penalized four minutes for drafting. I didn't find out about it until the next day when the times were posted. I remembered that a motorcycle had pulled up next to me while I was stuck in a group of six or seven riders. The red-haired, beady-eyed guy on the back of the cycle looked at me and started writing something in his notebook. I looked at the rider ahead of me. I thought I had been keeping enough distance, and as the official pulled away I wanted to yell after him, "Hey, I wasn't trying to draft. I'm not a cheater!"

It took me about 50 minutes to get to Verona, where I headed out on the 40-mile loop for the first time. I continued to pass people. To most of them I said "How's it going?" Some responded; some didn't. In order to make my goal of six hours on the bike, I knew I'd have to average approximately 18.5 miles per hour, so I kept a close eye on my speedometer while trying to monitor my strength.

At the second aid station I picked up a fresh bottle of water and another bottle of Gatorade as well as a couple of bananas. I choked down half of one of the three power bars I had in my pocket and washed it down with Gatorade. I felt strong and tried to keep pumping as hard as I could. The back side of the loop peaks out in the country before a speedy, 3-

mile descent into the little town of Cross Plains. I saw two or three bikers changing flats and one guy who must have wiped out—the side of his arm and his upper back were raw and bleeding.

The three toughest hills on the course lie halfway between Cross Plains and Verona. I was actually looking forward to the challenge of climbing them, knowing that there would be lots of people cheering on the sides of the roads at all three spots.

The first hill is about three-quarters of a mile in length and winds up through a tranquil wooded area. It's a hill that our group had used for some climbing practice earlier in the summer, so I felt very confident as I reached its base.

The second hill is a short, steep climb that local riders have affectionately named Bitch Hill. There were hundreds of people lining both sides of the road, and they crowded around me as I stood out of my saddle and crested the hill. This was reminiscent of scenes from the Tour de France except for the fact that I was moving about 3 miles an hour. Nevertheless, I was inspired to continue pushing hard.

From the top of Bitch Hill to the last climb is another few miles, and I knew that once the third climb was over, it would be a matter of minutes before I got to Verona and could start on the second loop. As I approached the final climb, I saw three guys in leopard skin thongs who were cooking over a Weber grill at the base of the hill. Next to the grill there was a lawn chair with some firewood stacked on it. Pinned to the back of the chair was a piece of paper with the name "Jeff" written on it. The guys jumped up and down and cheered as I came flying past. "You're looking great!" they yelled at me. "Keep it up! Last hill on the loop!"

When I got to Verona I was under three hours and still felt strong. The special needs bags were all piled at the side of the road outside Verona, and I pulled off to pick up the food I had packed. I had two bacon and egg sandwiches, a couple of salted nut rolls, some pretzels, and three gel packs just in case. I had a little trouble putting everything in my pocket and ended up throwing one of the sandwiches and salted nut rolls off to the side. Some of the people I remembered passing earlier zoomed by me, so I remounted the bike and tried to track them down.

On the second loop I settled into a comfortable pace with a small group of riders who were moving at the same speed. All the riders wore race numbers with their names on them, and I saw a familiar name ahead of me. As I pulled up next to him I realized it was Dr. O'Brien, the emergency room physician who had treated me two years earlier. He was riding a bike identical to mine. I said, "Hey, you probably don't remember me, but I saw you in the emergency room a couple of years ago and you gave me the name of the shop that sold me my bike."

"Yeah, I remember. How's it going?" he said.

"Great! I feel pretty good. How are you doing?"

"I'm hanging in there," he said.

I pulled away slowly and continued toward the back side of the loop for the second time. By now it was early afternoon and very warm. It was hard to gauge just how hot the day had become since the air dried my sweat so quickly and the winds made the temperature seem cooler than it actually was. I continued to drink every 15 minutes and occasionally poured water over the top of my helmet, letting it drip down my neck and back. My feet were a little numb, but they had been worse in the past, so I just ignored the numbness and pressed on. I knew that the last leg of the ride would be fast since it was mostly downhill with a trailing southwesterly wind. With just a few miles to go I pulled up alongside a young woman. "You know we're going to have to hustle to get back in less than six hours," I said.

"I know," she said. She obviously had the same time goal I did, and we both set to work to try to get back before 2:30.

As I approached the last 3-mile stretch I kept repeating to myself, "I love to run. I love to run. I can't wait to get off the bike. I love to run." This had become my new mantra to offset my real feelings—that I hated to run! And now the reality of the situation hit me. I was approaching the end of the second part of the race and had to steel myself for running a marathon.

The young woman who had been pacing me during the last part of the ride passed me a final time. Even though I tried, I couldn't stay with her. I cruised back into town and as I rounded the final corner of the ride, I saw Lake Monona and the Convention Center. I knew that I had less than a mile to go and about two minutes to get there to break six hours.

I should have slowed down a bit and tried to spin out my legs, but instead I pushed hard, and as I rolled up to the helix my watch read six hours and 20 seconds. I just barely missed my time goal, but I was satisfied with the ride. I circled up the helix, dismounted, crossed the timing mat, handed my bike to a volunteer, and took off for the bike-to-run changing room. I tried not to think about the fact that I still had 26.2 miles to go on my feet.

When I got off the bike my legs were tired, but I felt confident that I could still manage the run without too much trouble. I hurried into the bike-to-run changing area and started stripping off sweaty clothes. The sunscreen had worked well. Even though I had been sweating and dumping water on myself for six hours under a blazing hot sun, my body didn't feel burned anywhere. I also didn't smell very good. I peeled off my jersey and bibs and pulled on my running shorts. As I started stuffing things into a plastic bag, a volunteer came over. "I'll do that for you," he said. "Just get dressed and get going."

"Hey, thanks, man," I said. I pulled on a white sleeveless running shirt with my race number already pinned in place, put on my cap, laced up the shoes, and jogged through the piles of bags to the exit. I received another slathering of sunscreen and then ducked into a porta-potty. Since the beginning of the race I had not urinated once, which concerned me since I had consumed at least 10 bottles of Gatorade and water on the bike. I stood inside the john and forced out a small amount, then made my way from the Convention Center parking lot to the exit chute set up on Martin Luther King Boulevard. A noisy crowd that lined both sides of the finishing chute clapped and cheered for every runner who came out onto the course.

My plan was to run the first 30 minutes and then make stops at each aid station from that point onward. The first half mile of the run was an easy downhill section of State Street. My clothes were dry, my feet didn't ache, my legs had not cramped at all, and my stomach felt fine. I believed at that point that a four-and-a-half-hour marathon was a realistic possibility. At the top of State Street I saw my wife and kids and some friends who had come for the race. They let loose with a big cheer as I passed by. I heard Lisa tell our daughter, "He looks pretty good. See, he's smiling!"

I had previewed only the first 4 miles of the run course, and I didn't like the feeling of not knowing where the route was going to take me. When I got to the 2-mile marker I had already run for 19 minutes and was beginning to notice a problem that would dog me for the rest of the run. My bladder felt as though it was full, and continuing to run became uncomfortable. I stopped at the third aid station and drank some Gatorade, ate half a banana and a handful of pretzels, and dumped a cup of ice water over my head. I stepped quickly into a bathroom but couldn't get myself to pee. As soon as I left and started running again, the feeling that my bladder was full returned.

A lot of the runners who had started before me were struggling. Many were walking; others were moving along slowly, utilizing the infamous Ironman shuffle. I had not practiced the run/walk technique, but I knew that I was going to be forced to use it. I kept moving and wondered when I was going to get to the next mile marker. It seemed as though I had been going forever when I was surprised to come across mile marker 5. Somehow I had missed the two previous signs.

As I turned onto State Street, for a short stretch I was invigorated by the large number of people cheering. I noticed that everybody was trying to run during that stretch. I could only assume that, like me, they didn't want so many people to see them walking.

As I headed for the next stretch of the course it was obvious that many runners were struggling with the heat. One guy was hunched over, his hands on his knees, and vomiting onto the grass next to the sidewalk. It looked as though what was coming up was clear liquid, but he obviously wasn't going to be able to continue. Three minutes later when I went by the same place again, I saw him being helped into the back of an ambulance to be transported to a medical station. I tried not to think about how it would feel to be forced to abandon the race after so much training and preparation. I decided then that I would not push my body to the point where it would revolt and shut down. If I had to walk, I would walk. I was determined to finish the race.

I picked up the pace as I headed through the campus area along the south shore of Lake Mendota, and as I emerged from the trees onto a path that was decorated with hundreds of signs, I saw my coach and his wife up ahead. I certainly didn't want them to see me walking, so I forced myself into an uneasy run. When I came into view, Will jumped up and started yelling. "You're doing great, mate! You're looking strong, Dan! Awesome, buddy! Keep it up!" His wife snapped a couple of quick pictures as I ran by, and I think I tried to smile. When I got past them I had to stop and walk again.

Checking my watch, I realized that the winners of the race had more than likely already crossed the finish line. That was a distressing thought. I had 4 miles to go before I'd reach the dreaded turnaround, and I was not feeling very good. I made a point of stopping at every aid station to drink some kind of liquid and consume some salty food. I had not trained at all with salt tablets and didn't have any with me anyway, so I ate pretzels and drank chicken broth. Amazingly, as much as I ate and drank, my stomach never got bloated or nauseous. After stopping at another portable bathroom I noticed that there was a guy just ahead of me who had been stopping a lot too. As we walked through the aid station I said, "Have you been having trouble taking a leak?"

He said, "Yeah, it's really pissing me off." We both laughed.

"Do you think that's a bad sign?" I said.

He laughed again. "Yeah, I have a feeling that our kidneys have shut down."

"Hang in there," I said. "We're almost halfway there."

"You too."

I continued to walk, feeling frustrated that I couldn't make myself run for longer stretches of time. As I was coming back up Regent Street I saw a guy wearing a big puffy red, white, and blue wig. He was standing next to a street sign and screaming in pain. He'd lean on the pole trying to relax a stubborn cramp in the back of his leg. It was not the last time I would see him doing that.

A little farther along I saw Danny Montoya running very slowly. He was coming back up Regent Street the opposite direction from me. His head was down and he appeared to be really struggling. I shouted across the street, "Hey, Danny, keep pushing hard!" He either didn't hear me or was too weak to respond.

Running back up State Street for the first time was exciting, and I kept visualizing what it would feel like when I made it around again. I saw my cheering section near the Capitol, and they perked up when they spotted me and started yelling encouragement. I was trying to stay focused on running and had little energy to devote to waving back. I smiled and gave them half a wave. I didn't realize until later that I could have easily veered closer and given them all high fives, the way a bunch of other people were doing.

When I got to the Square, a couple of pros passed me. It looked as though even they were suffering, but at least they would be heading down the finishing chute in a minute or two. I finally got to the turnaround sign, somewhat disheartened by the knowledge that I was only halfway done with the marathon. I slowed down, circled the cone, and headed back out for another 13 miserable miles.

When I turned from the Capitol to head down State Street for the second time I knew that my goal of finishing in 12 hours was not going to happen. I saw that my cheering section had moved across to the north side of State Street, and when I ran past the group I yelled out to Lisa, "7:30!"

"What?" she said.

"It's going to be 7:30!" I said. She gave me a thumbs-up and I plodded on my way. I tried to run for five-minute chunks of time but found it to be impossible. I still had not been able to go to the bathroom, and as the day wore on this was the one physical issue that I worried might force me to quit. I had heard people say that strange things start happening to your body after 10 hours, and since I had rarely trained that long I wasn't sure what was happening or if there was anything I could do about it. All I knew is that it was very uncomfortable trying to run with a full bladder and maddening when I couldn't alleviate the problem. I stopped at 10 porta-potties before giving up on the idea.

Two of the women in my training group passed me with roughly 8 miles to go. "Hey, Dan, how's it going?"

"This is not fun anymore," I said. And I meant it.

Ordinarily I would have tried to stay with them and run at their pace, but at this point I didn't care who passed me. I just wanted to get to the next mile marker. I saw Pam Hollenhorst, the wife of one of my training buddies, and said "Where's John?" I had expected him to run me down long before this point in the race. She told me he was having stomach problems and that he was at least 30 minutes behind me. When I got to the bike path near the lake again, it was a relief to get out of the sun. Even though it was getting close to 6 o'clock, the air was still hot and every bit of shade was a relief. Will and his wife were still there. They acted as happy to see me as they had the first time I passed them. "Keep it up, mate!" Will yelled. "You're still doing great, Dan! You're looking strong!"

"Easy for him to say," I thought.

The line of runners continued to ebb and flow around me, and a lot of people were in the same condition as I was—they were alternately running and walking, with walking predominating. When I got to the steep hills on Observatory Drive I didn't see one person running.

I had already resigned myself to the fact that a 12-hour finish was not going to happen and at the start of the second half of the run had adjusted my goal to 12:30. At this point I realized that I wasn't even going to make that. I adjusted the goal again, promising myself that I would get to the finish line under 13 hours or die trying. It was exactly 7:05 when I passed the 22-mile marker, which gave me 54 minutes to cover the final 4.2 miles. I had decided in my mind that I would run the final mile, so when I finally got to the 25-mile marker I set off at an increased pace, determined to finish strong.

The crowds lining State Street were incredible, and even though hundreds of racers had already passed by, they shouted encouragement and clapped as if each one of us was in the lead. More than once during the race when my mind had retreated to a distant, happier place, I heard people yelling my last name. "Way to go, Madson! You're looking great, Madson!" Forgetting that I had my name pinned to my shirt, I kept thinking, "I wonder how all those people know my name."

I finally turned the corner and headed up State Street for the last time. I knew that Lisa would be at the finish line, so I pressed on and tried to focus on running hard. I passed the pile of special needs bags and at that point I could hear the announcer's voice over the loudspeaker system. There was a gap of a few seconds between me and the woman ahead of me, and when I looked back over my shoulder I saw three or four guys hustling up the block after me. I wanted to have the finishing chute to myself, so I picked up the pace a bit when I turned to the right and finally felt the elation of running down the green carpeting that led to the end. I had goose bumps and felt like crying and laughing at the same time as I heard the announcer say, "And from right here in Madison, Wisconsin, 44-year old Dan Madson! HEY, DAN! YOU'RE AN IRONMAN!!!" As two young women ran the tape back across the finish line, I raised my arms in the air and stepped across the final timing mat with the clock showing 12:56:41.

I had done it. I could now stand up and be counted with all the people before me who had trained and struggled to call themselves Ironmen. I was now one of them!

As soon as I crossed the line I caught Lisa's eye. She was working her way through the crowd to greet me. A volunteer hung a finisher's medal around my neck, and Lisa put her arms around me and gave me a hug. All I could say is, "I don't smell very good."

"That's OK," she said. "You did it! I'm so proud of you!"

I wanted to stay near the finish line for a while to cheer on some of the other finishers, but I knew that I had an appointment at home with an IV bag. And Lisa and I had already decided to do what I'm sure most Ironman finishers do, which was to . . .

Chapter 9
Invite Friends Over to Watch Recovery

Intravenous Rehydrating Can be Fun

I wasn't quite sure how I was supposed to feel after I crossed the finish line. I had seen some people finish the race looking fresh and happy while others collapsed in agony and exhaustion. A volunteer walked up to me and draped a silver warming blanket over my shoulders, asking me if I needed to sit down. "No," I said, "I just need something to drink."

"Come over here and I'll get you some water." He led me toward the medical tent where there were large buckets of bottled water, grabbed one, and gave it to me. "How do you feel?" he asked.

"I feel fine," was all I told him.

"Congratulations. You made it."

"Thanks. It was a long day. And thanks for your help, by the way. All of you volunteers were awesome today."

I walked back over to where Lisa and the kids were waiting and was surprised to see a bunch of our friends with curious smiles on their faces. "Way to go, Dan." "You did it." "How do you feel?" they asked.

Most of them knew that I had been training, and whenever we saw them they asked about how my racing was going. I shook hands with a couple of them and hugged a few others, all the while keeping an eye out for Glenn and Danny. I knew they had finished way ahead of me but hadn't seen either one of them in the crowd. Lisa escorted me over to a grassy section behind the bleachers, where I saw them both sitting. Glenn had a big smile on his face and looked fresh enough to go back out and do the course again. Danny looked beat. I was anxious to hear what had happened to him on the run. I only had one question. "What was your time, bro?" I asked him.

"Dude, I got so sick halfway through the run. I threw up three times and had to walk a lot. It was so hot."

I felt almost giddy by now. It was as though my body was in denial about what it had been put through. My legs didn't feel fatigued and my stomach felt fine. In fact, I was hungry and hoped there was some food handy. I still had the urge to urinate but couldn't see any porta-potties nearby to try one more time. I sat on the grass for half an hour and chatted briefly with everybody that had come to watch the race. I glanced up every now and then when I heard the announcer broadcast the name of another finisher. I didn't see anybody from my training group and assumed that most of them had finished ahead of me. After sitting for a while I started to get stiff, and even though it was still warm, I was chilled and started shivering.

I had been told by more than one Ironman finisher that it was helpful to receive an IV bag of saline solution to help with rehydration. As soon as Danny had finished the race he had been taken to the medical tent and weighed. The doctor discovered he had lost 14 pounds over the course of the day so he was given two bags of saline right away. I was not in desperate shape, and I didn't want to take attention away from somebody who might really need it. In addition, Lisa and I have a friend name Carrie who is an EMT, and she had offered to come to our house after the race and administer an IV in the privacy and comfort of my own living room.

We hiked back to our car around 9:15 and drove home. "How do you feel, bro?" Glenn asked.

"I'm disappointed with my time, but I feel all right." I said.

"Your time was great," Danny said, "I did my first Ironman in 12:45."

"Yeah, I guess you're right," I said. "I'm happy I finished, and I know that part of the reason I suffered on the run is that I didn't run hard enough in training. After the first half hour I just couldn't keep going."

"Hey, it's over now," said Glenn. "Let's go home and order some pizza and get something to drink."

When we arrived home the house was full of people. Along with our three kids and a couple of their friends, some friends from Salt Lake City were there and our EMT friend was as well. My knees and hips were stiff as I crawled out of the car and walked into the house. Lisa had already ordered pizza, and Danny and Glenn started eating immediately. I was feeling a little disoriented and sat down at the dining room table. "Let's get to it, Nurse Ratchett," I said to Carrie.

She got the IV bag ready and sat down next to me. "What happened to all your veins?" she said.

I looked at my arms and saw that my veins had collapsed. She took a tourniquet out of her bag and wrapped it around my bicep. "This oughta help get them to stand out again. Are you ready?"

"I guess so. Let's get it over with." Needles have never scared me, and I watched carefully as she finally found a spot to insert the needle and started to slide it slowly under the skin. As it disappeared into my vein, I started to feel sick. Even though I hadn't eaten anything in over two hours, I felt nauseous. All of a sudden my head seemed to weigh 50 pounds. It lolled slowly back and forth, and I could feel beads of sweat forming on my face and chest. "I gotta throw up," I mumbled.

"What did you say?" my wife asked, suddenly sounding concerned.

"I think I'm going to throw up," I said again, a bit more urgently. "Get me a bucket." She ran to the other side of the kitchen and grabbed a big cooking pot, ran back to the table, and set it on the floor in front of me. I closed my eyes and tried to keep my head from falling down on the table, but I was so dizzy I couldn't see straight. My head slowly dropped forward and banged onto the table as my right arm dropped lifelessly into my lap.

"Hey, you guys, let's get him over to the couch," Carrie said. Nobody moved.

"People, work with me!" my wife said. "He might be dying!" She came over and reached under my arms to help me stand up. I got to my feet and shuffled over to the couch, then lay down on my back. Everything in the room was still spinning, so I just closed my eyes and crossed my arms over my chest. I looked like Count Dracula reclining in his coffin. My daughter came over and peered over the back of the sofa. "Is he all right?" she asked. "He doesn't look so good."

I heard my oldest son say, "Are you sure he's still alive? He's white as a ghost."

"Hey, don't talk like that," my wife said. "They say a person's hearing is the last to go." While they were discussing my condition, my youngest son started taking pictures of me lying there. Carrie had been holding the IV bag above her head, and I heard her say that her arms were getting tired. "I brought a slow drip bag by mistake," she said. "This could take a while."

My wife suggested that they hang the bag from the balcony railing that was 12 feet over my head above the end of the couch. The drip line must have been long enough, because when I opened my eyes for a second I saw my son above me tying the bag to the railing. "Dad, are you going to be OK?" my daughter asked.

"Yeah, don't worry," I said, "I'm starting to feel a little better already." I lay there on the couch for over an hour while everybody else ate pizza and talked about the day. I heard everything but didn't feel like contributing to the merriment. I kept my eyes closed and I think even slept for a few minutes. I knew I must have been a pitiful sight, but I didn't care. I was attached to a drip line, and even if I had wanted to get up, I don't think I would have had the strength.

Slowly, minute by minute, I could feel my body perking up. It took well over an hour for the bag to empty completely. "Do you want me to hook up another bag?" Carrie asked.

"No, I don't think so. I want to get up and go to the bathroom." I felt better but was still weak and a bit disheveled as I headed to the bathroom. It was an immense relief to finally be able to go again, even though it hurt. It was nearly midnight and the first time I had urinated since 5 o'clock that morning. When I came out of the bathroom, everybody stopped talking and looked at me. "Is there any pizza left?" I asked.

"Hey, bro, you're looking better," Danny said with a laugh. "We thought we might lose you for a minute there."

"Don't say that," my wife said.

"I just need some food," I repeated. I think that when I took that first bite of cold pizza I had never tasted anything so good. I wolfed down the three pieces that remained in the box and washed them down with an ice-cold Corona. I perked up visibly after getting something in my stomach and started asking questions. "Dude, what happened to you on the run?" I said to Danny.

"I don't know. I just wanted to lie down in the grass and take a nap. I had no energy at all. I threw up three times in garbage cans and must have been having the same problem you were having."

"So what was your time?" I asked.

"11:20," he said.

"What about you?" I asked Glenn.

"10:53," he said.

"That's amazing," I said. "One of you is undertrained and overweight and the other one gets sick on the run, and you both still clobbered me."

"You had a great finish for your first Ironman," Danny said. "You'll be faster next year."

At this point I honestly didn't think that I would do Ironman again, but I also knew that I wouldn't have much time to . . .

Chapter 10
Collect Some Post-Race Thoughts

From "I Will Never Do This Again" to "Yes, I Signed Up for Next Year"

Ironman races are so popular these days that if you want to compete in one you have to be ready to register the minute it opens. When I went to bed early Monday morning, I was exhausted and had experienced enough suffering during the day to wonder if this was a distance worth repeating. Glenn and Danny had enjoyed the week at our house, loved the course, and were amazed at the atmosphere and great community support. "Dude, we're both coming back next year," Glenn said before he went to bed. I didn't say anything because I wasn't sure what I wanted to do.

The next morning I got up at 8 o'clock and the house was still quiet. I had a little trouble walking down the steps because my knees were still sore, and when I got to the kitchen Danny was already sitting at the table reading the morning paper and drinking a cup of coffee. "Good morning, Rookie."

"How's it going, bro? Where's Glenn?" I asked.

"He'll be up soon," he said.

By mid-morning, bodies were starting to appear from various parts of the house. Everybody was dragging from consecutive late nights and an emotional day.

Glenn, Danny, and I returned to the Convention Center early Monday afternoon for a final time to attend the post-race banquet and awards ceremony. I was intrigued to find out how the Hawaii roll-down went as well. I knew that I had no chance to qualify unless well over a hundred people who had finished ahead of me in my age group all got deathly ill or decided to decline the invitation.

"What kind of turnout do they get for the awards lunch?" I asked.

"Usually it's very good," Danny said.

"The food is great," said Glenn. It turned out that they were both right. The main hall of the Convention Center was packed with circular tables, and we had a hard time finding three seats together. The food was excellent. After we ate, we settled back to watch the awards presentation. Dave Harju repeated as the male winner, while Nicole DeBoom won the women's division. All the age-group winners were recognized, and one woman from my training group got a top-three finish and an invitation to Hawaii.

After the ceremony concluded, we stood in line to receive the final results sheets and the footage that had been shot the day before, which was passed out on DVD to everybody. We stopped at the photo shop and bought some of the pictures that had been taken, then headed back home. As we were about to exit the Convention Center, Glenn and Danny stopped, turned around, and started back toward the on-site registration booth. Both had brought their checkbooks and were intent on registering for the race for the following year. I didn't have my checkbook with me, so I told them I would think about it on the way home. "You'll feel better soon, bro," Danny said. "You'll want to do it again next year, I promise you."

"I'll check out the website when I get home and decide then," I said.

When we got home I walked into Lisa's office and sat down at the computer. "So, are you going to do it again next year?" she asked.

"I don't know," I said.

"You have my blessing if you want to keep training hard. I want you to have something to be passionate about." She walked over and plopped a credit card down on the desk in front of me. "Don't be such a wuss," she said. Glenn and Danny started laughing.

"Yeah, don't be such a wuss, Rookie," Glenn said.

I clicked on the Ironman website, grabbed the credit card, and filled out the application for the following year. I knew it was a decision that I would be glad I had made once my body recovered and I started working out again.

The week had been eventful and enjoyable, but all good things must come to an end. Danny's flight left for the airport late Monday afternoon. Glenn and I dropped him off and gave him a hug. "Thank you so much for the place to stay and a great week," Danny said. "I can't wait to come back next year, bro."

"Thanks for coming," I said. "It was a tremendous week, and it'll be better next year."

"Have a safe trip home. See you when I get back," Glenn said.

Glenn and his wife were scheduled to leave on Tuesday morning, and the farewell would be repeated one more time the next day.

It had been a memorable week of training, eating, racing, laughing, and recovering. There was nothing left to do but . . .

Chapter 11
Take a Vacation to Hawaii

Would You Like Another
Mai-Tai, Mr. . . . Keliikipi?

My wife had scheduled a trip to Hawaii earlier in the year that would be partly for business and partly for pleasure. She had originally planned on leaving Monday morning, but I told her that might not be such a good idea since I wasn't sure if I would be in any condition to travel the day after Ironman. I also told her that I wanted to attend the post-race activities on Monday afternoon, so she rescheduled our flight for 9 o'clock on Tuesday morning, knowing that would give me an extra day to recover. Before leaving for New Mexico, Glenn had warned me, "You may not start to feel stiff until two days after the race," he said. His prediction turned out to be right.

Monday was a busy day with the awards event, a trip to the airport, and the job of getting all our gear cleaned up and organized. Lisa and I didn't finish packing for Hawaii until 1:30 in the morning and crawled into bed knowing that it would be another short night. We thought that our flight to Hawaii left at the same time as Glenn's flight to New Mexico and that we all had to get to the airport by 6:00 A.M. We didn't have enough room in my vehicle for four people, a bike box, and all our luggage, so I hired a cab for Glenn and his wife.

When we got up Tuesday morning, Lisa called to confirm our flight times and discovered that our departure had been changed from 7:00 to 9:00 A.M. With that extra bit of leeway I was able to run Glenn and his wife to the airport and then return to pick up Lisa. She likes to get to the airport two hours before a flight is scheduled to leave while I prefer to get there with as little time to spare as possible. We usually argue about it, compromise, and get there two hours early.

While waiting to board our flight, I drank a cup of coffee and read the morning paper that I had grabbed from the mailbox on the way out of the driveway. Walking down the hallway of the terminal was a painful exercise, as the muscles in my legs finally figured out what I had done to them and decided to be sore in direct proportion to the punishment they had incurred. My quadriceps were especially tender, and I felt twinges of muscular cramping waiting to happen in my calves and hamstrings as well. Lisa had upgraded our coach tickets to first class on the longest leg of our trip from Minneapolis to Honolulu, but I was not looking forward to the cramped seats from Madison to Minneapolis and from Honolulu to Maui. I proudly wore a black T-shirt with the Ironman Wisconsin logo in bright red on the front. As we boarded the first plane, a flight attendant looked at my shirt. "Did you do Ironman on Sunday?" she asked.

"Yes, I did," I said.

"Oh, that's so cool. My boyfriend's boss's daughter did it too. I just think it's so awesome to be able to do something like that. How did you finish?"

"I finished in 12:56," I said. "It wasn't as fast as I had hoped to do, but I'm happy with it."

"You should just be happy you finished," she said. "Congratulations!"

"Thanks, dude," I said.

My wife looked over at me. "You shouldn't call a female flight attendant 'dude,'" she said.

"Yeah, sorry," I told her. "Bad habit."

The morning was clear and cool as we took off for Minneapolis, and I settled in for the short flight. It turned out to be longer than I expected. I was sitting in an aisle seat with my legs splayed and my left knee sticking out in the aisle. I put my head back and closed my eyes, hoping the caffeine I had ingested earlier would not prevent me from dozing off. I had just entered that blissful pre-sleep daze that feels so good when the flight attendant wheeled her cart down the aisle to start dispensing drinks at the back of the plane. Not noticing that my knee was blocking her way, she rammed the corner of the cart directly into it. I yelled "OUCH!" and involuntarily retracted my leg from the aisle. The quick movement triggered a spasm in my left calf muscle and hamstring, and both muscles seized up instantly. I grabbed the back of my left leg and tried to straighten it, but the cart was in the aisle and the seat in front got in the way. "My leg is cramping!" I cried.

"Are you all right, sir?" the flight attendant asked. "Is there anything I can do?"

"Move your cart so I can straighten my leg," I told her. As soon as she pushed the cart past my seat I turned to stand up in the aisle in an effort to stretch my left leg. She stopped quickly to see if I was OK, and in doing so knocked an open can of tomato juice off the top of the cart right into the lap of the man sitting behind me. He jerked upright as the cold liquid spilled down him. As the flight attendant cleaned up the mess behind me, I hopped up and down in the aisle in an effort to ease the cramps. Finally they relaxed enough so I could take my seat again, and I spent the rest of the trip with my left leg extended into the aisle hoping that the cramps would not reappear.

The eight-hour flight from Minneapolis to Honolulu was uneventful. We had two great meals, and both of us slept a good deal of the way. Our plan was to stay on the island of Maui for three days and see some friends who were going to be there at the same time. We rented a condo between Lahaina and Wailea and spent time relaxing, sightseeing, and hanging out with our friends.

On Wednesday afternoon I decided to go for my first recovery swim in the ocean. My legs were quite sore by this point, and I hoped a warm ocean swim would be therapeutic. Lisa said, "I don't know if it's a good idea for you to go swimming in the ocean. What if you get attacked by a shark? Or a giant jellyfish? What happens if a riptide takes you out to sea?"

"I'll swim parallel to shore and you can spot me as I go."

"Can't I watch you from my chair?" she said.

"That's fine with me," I said.

"Be careful about those boats that are out there!" she yelled as I walked toward the water.

I didn't have my wet suit with me, and I was pleasantly surprised at how buoyant the salt water was. I picked out the mast of a sailboat moored about 1,000 yards away down the beach and set off. Swimming in salt water took some getting used to, but I didn't mind it even as I occasionally swallowed some of the briny stuff. The surf was relatively calm that afternoon, and the mild swells gently lifted my body up and down as I pulled toward my target. I didn't see any sharks or jellyfish and had no run-ins with boaters. The tide was nonexistent, so the only thing that concerned me was the occasional coral reef that came into view in the shallow water. Every so often the swells would drop me down low enough for my hands to scrape the top of the coral. I weaved through the coral beds and managed to avoid being dragged along the tops of their craggy peaks.

When I got back to where Lisa was sitting, my tongue was slightly swollen from the 45-minute exposure to salty water and I was dying for a drink of fresh water. "How was your swim?" Lisa asked.

"It was great except for the sharks and jellyfish I ran into," I said. "Oh, yeah, and that riptide that nearly dragged me out to sea."

"Very funny, Mr. Ironman," she said.

I grabbed a bottle of water from her beach bag and gulped it down before washing off the salt water under a beach shower. It had been invigorating to swim again after three days of sitting around. My arms and shoulders had that familiar and satisfying feeling of fatigue, and even my legs felt better.

We flew to Honolulu on Friday afternoon and were met at the airport by one of my wife's business associates, a native of the island of Oahu whose last name was Keliikipi. I couldn't pronounce the name very well and neither could Lisa, so we just tried to avoid having to say it. Jahnelle drove us to the Hilton Hawaiian Village on Waikiki Beach and checked us in under her name because she was able to get a discounted rate. We were shown to a suite on the 21st floor with a gorgeous view of the ocean in both directions. That night we ate dinner at a waterfront restaurant and reminisced about the events of the past two weeks.

"So, are you happy I made you sign up for Ironman next year?"

"You didn't make me," I said.

"Well, you didn't sound like you wanted to do it again," she said.

"I just wanted to have a little time to think about it, that's all. It fills up so fast that I don't even have a couple of days to make up my mind."

"But are you happy now that you're in?"

"Sure. I know I'll feel a lot better in a few days and then I'll thank you for making me sign up. I promise."

The next morning we decided to spend the day at the beach. I set up two chairs in the sand near the water and went to check out some towels at a nearby kiosk. A young Hawaiian was working behind the counter. When I asked him for some towels, he said, "What's your room number, sir?"

"2153," I said.

"How many towels would you like, Mr. . . . ."

He paused for a second and looked away from the computer in order to get a better look at me. "How many towels would you like, Mr. Key-lee-ee-key-pee?" Then, after a slight pause, he said, "Are you Hawaiian?"

"No, actually I'm Norwegian," I told him.

"There's a football player for the University of Hawaii with the same last name. Are you related to him?"

"No, I don't think so," I told him. "I'd like four towels please."

"Sure. Here you go, Mr. . . . Keliikipi." He said the last name very slowly again as he handed me the towels. "Have a nice day."

I put the towels on our chairs and then walked back to the bar to pick up a couple of drinks. We had been sitting there for an hour or so when a bartender stopped by to pick up our glasses and see if we wanted refills. "Care for another mai-tai, Mr. and Mrs. . . . Keliikipi? You don't look Hawaiian. Are you from here?" he asked when he got a closer look at us.

"Actually, we're from Wisconsin," my wife explained.

"It's a long story. I'm Norwegian and she's German," I said. "And, yes, we both would like another mai-tai."

That afternoon, while Lisa was getting ready for dinner, I went for a 30-minute run along the ocean. I ran at a very easy pace and tried to coax some life back into my tender legs. As hard as I had trained before Ironman and as tired as I was afterward, I knew it wouldn't be long before my body and mind would be completely recovered. I had convinced myself that I could perform much better the second time around. I knew how to train; I knew what to eat; I knew how to pace myself for a long day of racing. I could hardly wait to get home and start training again.

Afterword

If you asked a hundred Ironman triathletes what made them want to do something so difficult, you would get a hundred different answers. I enjoy the solitary nature of training. I feel good physically and mentally when I'm in great shape. I like planning for races and trying to achieve a time goal. I like chasing lower numbers. I enjoy the people who are involved in the sport and like talking to them about their backgrounds and experiences. What I like best, however, is the joy of packing a gym bag and heading off to practice the way I used to when competing in high school and college.

I vividly remember the first organized sports practice I ever attended. I was eight years old and was signed up to play little league baseball in my hometown in southwestern Minnesota. On the morning of the first practice I hung my baseball glove over the handlebar of my bike and rode to the baseball fields. It was a hot day in early June, and we practiced for two hours that morning on a dusty field under a blazing sun—and I loved every minute of it. I rode home that day exhausted, covered with dirt, and as happy as I had ever been. From that day forward I never got tired of going to practices, preparing for games, and competing against others as hard as I could. I tried not to gloat when we won; I rarely cried when we lost. I just reveled in the pleasure of competition, of learning and perfecting new skills, of pushing myself to new limits.

A lot of people who talk to me about my Ironman experience think I'm crazy. Some are impressed. Most make the same comments, like "I could never do something like that. I get tired walking up the stairs."

Triathlon is a wonderful sport. More than that, it's a way of living embraced by a rather unique subculture of the human species—people who enjoy a lifestyle of elevated fitness, the camaraderie of their training groups, and the never-ending excitement of competition.

In October 2002, as I commenced training for my foray into the world of triathlon and Ironman Wisconsin, I adopted the slogan "Only the Strong Survive." Well, I did it. I survived. I am an Ironman!